Dolls
Dressmaking

MILNER CRAFT SERIES

Dolls
Dressmaking

MARILYN CARTER

My Favourite Things

SALLY MILNER PUBLISHING

DEDICATION

This book is dedicated to my late father 'Mick', a very proud father

First published in 1993 by
Sally Milner Publishing Pty Ltd
588 Darling Street
Rozelle NSW 2039 Australia

Reprinted 1993

© Marilyn Carter 1993

Design layout by Gatya Kelly, Doric Order
Illustrations by Anna Warren
Photography by Andre Martin
Typeset in Australia by Asset Typesetting Pty Ltd
Printed in Australia by Impact Printing, Melbourne

National Library of Australia Cataloguing-in-Publication data:

Carter, Marilyn A.
    Dolls Dressmaking.

    ISBN 1 86351 078 8.
    1. Dolls clothes. I. Title. (Series:
Milner craft series).

745.59221

CONTENTS

ACKNOWLEDGEMENTS

My thanks go to all my family and close friends who encouraged me when the seed was planted for a book on *Dolls Dressmaking*.

My heartfelt thanks to my Mum for her beautiful crochet. My thanks also to:

- My friend Elaine Glanville for the use of her beautiful home and antique furniture used in photography
- Maureen and Barry Brown of Pots Plus for their help and encouragement and models
- Margaret Handley for supplying models
- Diana Oakley from Needlecraft International for her help in choosing fabrics and laces
- Beth from Needlecraft International for her exquisite embroidery which finished off the projects
- Wendy Strickland for her beautiful smocking
- Jenny Haskins for her encouragement and self confidence lessons
- Mary McLure for her beautiful pram
- Pfaff Australia Pty Ltd
- DMC Threads for all threads
- Les Ripper from Helmar Products
- Rokset Industries for the Olfa products, and
- Jennifer Esteban for providing such a beautiful young lady to grace the cover of my book

Marilyn Carter

INTRODUCTION

Dressing dolls has been a hobby of mine since I was twelve years old and my mother gave me a Barbie doll for Christmas: I was hooked on dressing her.

I would hop on my bike with a basket of goodies and visit my aunt to go through her scrap bag from the dressmaking she did for her daughters. My mother would do all the knitting and crochet for Barbie while I sewed.

With the wonderful sewing machines available today, I can design my own stitches and outfits. They are one-of-a-kind and I am pleased to share them with you.

The dolls I have used for my models are:

Jennifer Esteban's 'Camille' — 63 cm (25″)
JDK's 'Hilda' — 40 cm (16″)
SFBJ 'Twirp' — 25cm (10″)
Hildegarde Gunzel's 'Sleeping Jenny' — 40 cm (16″)
Heubach's 'Johan' — 45 cm (18″).

WHERE TO BEGIN

The choice of fabric makes a great difference to the end result of your doll's outfit. If you mix colours, make sure they are coordinated, and always consider the size of the print in the fabric in relation to the size of the doll. For instance, you would not put a medium to large print on a small doll; a very dainty print would be more appropriate.

Remember you are dressing your dolls to be dainty, not gaudy and overpowering.

If you are dressing fantasy dolls, you can let your head go and experiment.

Larger dolls can have small prints or medium prints, again relating to the size of the doll.

Accessories for your doll should be chosen carefully — it is important to have the right type of shoes and socks, booties for baby dolls, fashion shoes for reproduction dolls. In dressing reproduction dolls, whether French or German, make sure their shoes and socks are related to their origin.

Hats are a lovely finish for dolls. There are lots to choose from: hoop bonnets, straw hats, baby bonnets and rushed bonnets. With patience and practice anyone can learn to make the right type of hat.

EQUIPMENT AND ESSENTIAL TOOLS

- Sewing machine: cleaned and oiled. To clean your machine really well, spray 'Dust Away' or a similar product around the bobbin area, needle bar and into the top tension disc area to blow the dust out. It is surprising how much dust and fluff can accumulate in a machine.

  The machine should be oiled with one drop of oil.

  Change the needle when necessary: remember needles have a sewing life of 6 hours.

- Overlocking machine: cleaned and oiled. Use 'Dust Away' or a similar product to clean your overlocker, as these machines get extremely fluffy. Oil your machine.

- Universal needles for sewing machines: sizes 60-80 depending on fabric

- Universal stretch needles for sewing machine for stretch fabric: size 75

- Olfa board and small rotary cutter

- Handsewing needles

- Pins: glass head or lace pins

- Good pair of dressmaking scissors

- Small embroidery scissors

- Fabric marking pen (blue)

- Fray Stoppa or similar fabric glue

- Fabric stabiliser

- Tracing paper for patterns (I like greaseproof lunch paper)

- Paper scissors

- Pencil

- Tape measure (essential)

- Fabrics: voiles, batiste, silk, flannel, wool challis, polycotton

- Laces: many different types, preferably cotton

- Ribbons: double-sided satin eliminates the problem of which way the bow sits

- Fasteners: hooks and eyes, 000 press studs, buttons

- Elastic: hat elastic, and 3 mm (⅛″) flat

- Threads: DMC broder cotton 50 for all French heirloom methods
DMC polycotton for dressmaking
DMC embroidery thread for all your embroidery
Invisible thread

TRIMS AND FINISHES

There are many different ways of trimming dolls clothes, as you may have noticed if you have been to doll shows. Here are some of the different types of trim.

- **Pintucks** (sometimes called airtucks) are made using a twin needle and a pintucking foot for your machine. Set your machine up for pintucking and insert twin needle. When threading your machine for twin needle work, make sure that you have the left needle thread going anti-clockwise and the right needle thread going clockwise. The left thread runs on the left side of your tension disc and the right thread runs on the right side of the tension disc. Thread the left thread into the left needle and the right thread into the right needle. Press twin needle button if you have this on your machine. To have lovely crisp pintucks, spray starch your fabric at least twice before you are ready to start your pintucks.

    If you are pintucking a bodice or sleeves, pintuck a square of fabric first before cutting out, as pintucks reduce the size of the fabric piece. If pintucking around skirts, always add a little extra to the length.

    Pintucks may be given a shadow of colour by cording them with coloured cordonnet thread. This looks very effective on an all-white outfit as the touch of colour in the pintucks softens the overall effect.

- **Tucks** — these may be of different widths, depending on the size of the dress. Press along the centre fold of the tucks and stitch precisely the same width along the fold of fabric, whether it be 6 mm (¼″), 12 mm (½″) or 25 mm (1″) in from folded edge. The width depends on the size of the doll and the style of the dress.

    A secret to pintucks and tucks is that you must always be on the straight of the grain in your fabric. By doing this you will always have perfectly straight pintucks or tucks. Pull one thread to start you off on the straight grain.

- **Hand embroidery** — this is a lovely finish for dolls clothes. I always like to use DMC embroidery threads as they have a beautiful colour range to choose from.

- **Smocking** — is a rewarding finish for your dolls clothes. You can devote as much time to smocking a piece as you might take to assemble your garment. There are so many beautiful patterns to choose from, not only for girls outfits but also boys.

- **Bows** — use to finish off the back of your dolls dresses or pinafores. You can choose from silk ribbon, satin double-sided ribbon or satin single-sided ribbon.

- **Tassles** — embroidery thread or fine crochet thread is ideal for tassles. Cut a piece of cardboard a little longer than the required length of your tassel and wind thread around cardboard until you have the thickness you require. Thread a piece of the same thread through all the thicknesses at one end of the cardboard. Tie into a knot (do not cut thread). Cut through the thicknesses at the other end of the cardboard. Bring the thread used to tie the knot down into the tassle and wind a separate piece of thread around the end four or five times. Tie off with a firm knot. Slip a thread through the end of the tassle to use for attaching the tassle. Trim the cut ends evenly.

- **Rosettes** — to make different sized rosettes, it is simply a matter of using ribbons of different widths. To create a basic rosette, run thread along one edge of your ribbon and pull up the thread to form rosettes as shown in the diagram.

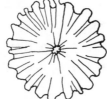

Basic rosette

A variety of other rosettes can be created by following the methods described below.

Sew a running stitch by hand in a zigzag pattern along the length of ribbon and pull up to form gathers in ribbon. Join ends to form a circle and stitch together. If you sew your running stitches closer together, this will give a smaller, tighter shirring effect and if you sew them further apart, this will give a looser shirring effect (see diagrams).

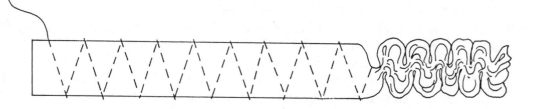

Zigzag stitching for tighter rosette variation

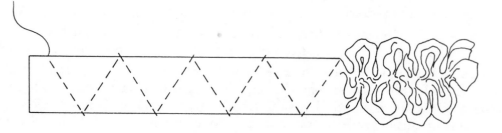

Zigzag stitching for looser rosette variation

- **Shirred ribbon** — run a row of stitches by hand along each edge of the ribbon and pull up. Another method is to run a row of stitches along the centre of the ribbon and pull up to give the gathered effect you require. (See diagrams.)

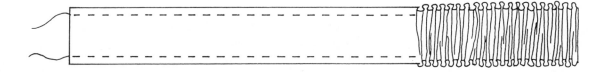

Shirring ribbon using two rows of running stitch

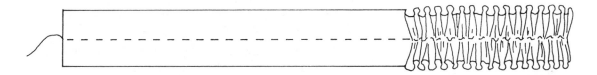

Shirring ribbon using one centre row of running stitch

- **Shell edging by hand** — this edging looks lovely around sleeve edges, neck edges and hems. Working from the wrong side of your garment, fold over the required hem and run three small straight stitches in the fold of the fabric, taking the needle underneath to the right side and coming back up into the edge of the fold. Pull the thread firmly to form the shell pattern, and do a second overstitch to make it firm. Repeat this procedure until completed. (See diagram.)

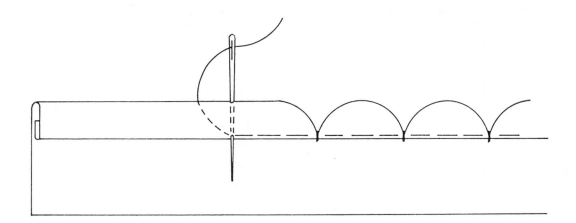

Shell edging by hand

MEASURING DOLLS

The height of a doll is measured from the top of the head to the toe. Chest measurements are essential for baby dolls as their chests are wider. Inside and outside leg measurements are necessary for trouser or short patterns for boy or girl dolls.

Always measure your doll from centre front and back of the neck to waist for bodice, and from centre front and back neck to midway of armholes for yokes.

For longer waisted dresses, extend the bodice measurement to required length of long-waisted bodice and widen slightly from armhole to desired length as you will need more width in hip area.

Shoulder to wrist measurement for sleeve length: if you want long sleeves over bent arms, measure arm with bend in elbow to allow for extra length.

Skirt measurement should be from waist or hip to desired length of skirt, allowing for hem.

Centre back down to crotch and up to centre front measurement is for depth of panties and trousers or shorts.

ADJUSTING YOUR PATTERNS

You may use one pattern for several different dolls by adjusting to suit the shape of your doll. Baby dolls tend to have much bigger chests and you must always allow for this when making a pattern or adjusting one to fit.

Cloth body dolls vary a lot in size, as no two people fill a cloth body in exactly the same way.

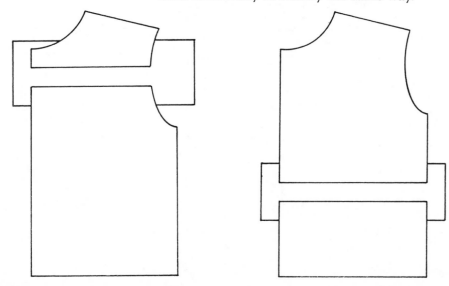

Lengthening bodice from shoulder to armhole   Lengthening bodice from underarm to waistline

- **Lengthening bodice pattern** — always check where you need to lengthen, either from shoulder to underarm section, or underarm to waistline or hipline section.

- **Sleeves** — to vary for fullness, remember that if you want a much fuller head in the sleeve, you must add more in the width and the height as in diagram. Slash down sleeve pattern to near edge, spread to desired fullness and continue shape of sleeve at head of pattern. This will give you the fullness at top and underarm without changing width of sleeve edge.

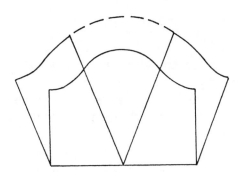 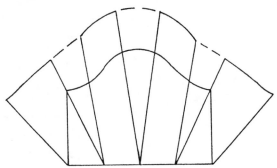

Adjusting sleeves for a fuller head

To achieve all-over fullness, slash pattern down centre of sleeve all the way through. Place the two pieces of sleeve pattern on top of another piece of paper, measure how much extra you would like to add from centre of one side to other side, making sure this measurement is accurate from top of sleeve to edge of sleeve, as in diagram.

Now you must add more height to this sleeve adjustment. If you don't add the height, your sleeve will drag across top of shoulder.

Adjusting sleeves for all-over fullness

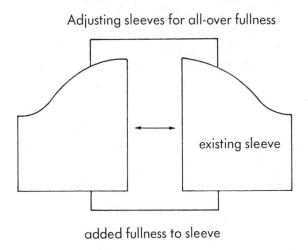 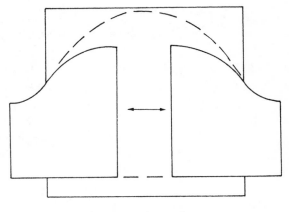

existing sleeve

added fullness to sleeve

added height to sleeve

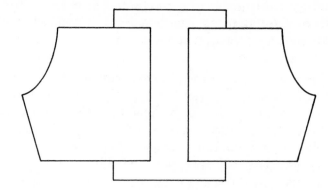

Adjusting panties for greater fullness

- **Panties** — if panties are the right size but a little tight, slash pattern down the side and add into side the extra fullness you would like. Some baby bodies are fatter than others but not necessarily as long so you need to add extra fullness.

- **Skirts** — always check pattern length against your doll, whether it is a waistline skirt or a drop waist skirt. If you find you have miscalculated your skirt length, there are a number of methods of recovering to deal with this problem.

  If you are using lots of lace in your dress, you can always add more insertion lace into the skirt or a wider edge lace to bottom of skirt. Stitch a panel of pintucking and insert this in with insertion lace.

  If you are using a small print, you may like to add a plain strip of colour on the edge of the skirt to match the colour in the print.

  To give extra fullness in skirt, e.g. christening dresses, party dresses and yoke style dresses, use the full width of fabric.

- **Hems on skirts** — hand stitch your hem if no stitching is desired on right side.

  Edge lace can be used to finish off length of skirt.

  A double skirt with the fold of fabric at the hemline eliminates any type of hemming.

  If you have a circular skirt, stitch insertion lace to edge and turn up a small amount of fabric; pull up passive thread in head of lace until your hem sits neatly in place. This method eliminates having to run a gathering thread around your hem in a circular skirt and pulling up to fit, and it is a very neat finish.

  Always cut selvedges away before cutting fabric out.

- When making buttonholes, always put two (2) layers of greaseproof paper underneath as this allows the fabric to feed through evenly.

PREPARING CLOTH BODIES

There are different types of cloth bodies.

- Baby dolls have only porcelain head and hands and have a complete soft body.
- Fashion dolls have shoulder plate, head, arms and half legs put onto a kid leather body, which gives a beautiful shape.
- Modern dolls usually have a cloth body with full porcelain arms and legs.

I suggest using calico or homespun fabric for your bodies. The fleecy stretch fabric which has been used tends to stretch out of shape when you fill the body. There is much more stability in woven fabrics such as calico and homespun. Homespun comes in a range of colours from which you can choose.

When using calico or homespun, I suggest using a strong quilting thread to stitch with, as it is much stronger than polycotton thread. When putting arms and legs into the bodies, use the quilting thread to tie around on the outside as well and use PVA Craft Hobby glue from Helmar or similar.

When putting heads on the bodies, use a couple of strands of quilting thread or crochet thread to tie around the neck. I only occassionally put glue on the neck, as it is nice to be able to turn the head when positioning the doll.

Never skimp when cutting out bodies: to do so will prevent them from sitting properly. Always cut out to the instructions given with body patterns.

TWIRP

A 25 cm (10 inch) DOLL WITH A PORCELAIN BODY

Everyone loves small dolls. You can make a beautiful collection of these dolls, whether they are Millettes or childlike dolls such as our little 'Twirp'. A pretty hailspot dress and apron make her an irresistible addition to your collection. Her shoes and socks are commercially made and are available at most doll shops. You may prefer to knit her some socks and make her shoes.

MATERIALS

25 cm (10") hailspot fabric for dress and panties
15 cm (6") white batiste for apron
1 m (40") of 10 mm (⅜") narrow edge lace (for panties, dress and apron)
hat elastic
DMC polycotton thread — white
white embroidery thread (machine)
fabric stabiliser spray (Helmar or similar)
DMC embroidery thread — colours 818 pink and 524 green (for apron and bonnet)
size 000 studs or small buttons for dress
size 000 studs for apron

METHOD

Using pattern supplied, cut:
   2 front bodices on fold
   2 back bodices on fold
   2 sleeves
   1 dress skirt on fold
   2 panties

PANTIES

- Attach lace to legs using whip and roll method, i.e. zigzag W3.5 L1.
- With right sides of fabric together, sew centre front and centre back seams together.

- Finish off top raw edge of panties using roll and whip method (zigzag W3.5 L1), turn over 6 mm (¼″) to make a casing, and stitch in place, leaving an opening to thread elastic through casing.

- Join crotch seam. Apply Fray Stoppa or similar fabric glue to threads at ends of crotch seam before cutting away.

- Using zigzag W3 L2, stitch over hat elastic around inside of legs 12 mm (½″) from fabric edge. Do not cut a short length of elastic to do this — it makes it too difficult to manage. When you have stitched elastic in place, pull up to fit leg (elastic should pull freely through zigzag). Secure elastic, then cut away remaining length.

- Repeat for other leg.

- Cut elastic to fit waist, thread through casing at top of panties and secure.

DRESS

- Join shoulder seams of front bodices to back bodices as shown in diagram.

- Press centre backs on foldline.

- Measure neck edge from centre back around front neckline to centre back. Double this measurement and cut narrow edge lace to this length.

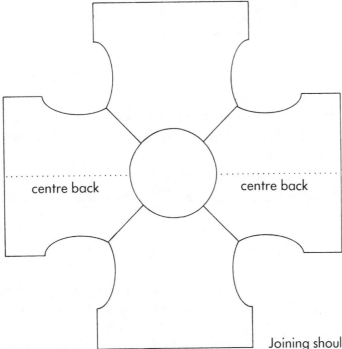

centre back   centre back

Joining shoulder seams of front and back bodices

- Pull up passive thread in head of lace to gather to fit neckline from centre back to centre back.
- Fold over ends of lace double and stitch lace around neckline on seam line, keeping facing free.
- Bring right side of facings to right side of bodice, matching shoulder seams.
- Stitch around neckline on previous stitching line from centre back around to centre back.
- Clip around neckline, turn right side out and press.

SLEEVES

- Attach lace to sleeve edges using whip and roll method (see panties above). Press.
- Run two rows of gathering stitches around top of sleeve and fit into open armholes, right sides together, pull up gathers to fit, and stitch together, keeping facing free.
- Repeat for other sleeve.
- With right sides of sleeves and bodices together, stitch underarm seam from sleeve edge through to side seam of bodice as in diagram.

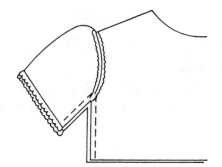

Stitching underarm seam

- Stitch side seams of bodice facing together and turn inside to conceal facing side seam.
- Clip where necessary around armhole seams and facing armholes.
- Turn in hem on armhole facing, matching shoulder and side seam, and slip stitch facing around armholes, turning in as you go.
- Attach hat elastic to inside of sleeves as for legs of panties.
- Apply Fray Stoppa or similar fabric glue to any loose threads at sleeves before cutting away.

SKIRT

- Finish raw edges of back seam using roll and whip method (zigzag W3.5 L1) and stitch back seam from dot to hem. Run two rows of gathering stitches around top of skirt.
- Fold back seam allowance to wrong side on both sides of back seam.

- Match centre front of skirt to centre front of bodice and back foldlines of bodice to back openings on skirt, keeping bodice facing free.
- Pull up gathering threads to fit skirt to bodice, distributing gathers evenly.
- Stitch skirt to bodice, keeping bodice facing free.
- Trim seam, fold up hem on bodice facing, matching side seams of bodice, and slip stitch facing to seam that joins skirt to bodice.
- Try the dress on your doll to check the length of the skirt. Mark hemline, finish off raw edge of hem using roll and whip method (zigzag W3.5 L1), turn up required width of hem and slip stitch in place.
- Make buttonholes by machine or hand, run Fray Stoppa or similar fabric glue down centre of buttonholes with a pin, let dry and cut with embroidery scissors.
- Sew buttons down back where shown on pattern. If you prefer to use press studs, use size 000.

APRON

We are going to make our own edge for the apron, or you may like to purchase lace.

METHOD FOR SCALLOP EDGE OF SKIRT AND SHOULDER

RUFFLES

Using patterns supplied, cut out apron skirt.

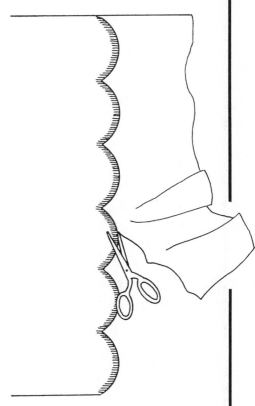

- Spray stabiliser about 50 mm (2″) from bottom raw edge; let dry and press — fabric will become stiff.
- Sew a scalloped edge on this bottom raw edge as follows. Most sewing machines have a satin stitch scallop of some description. Using the scallop stitch on the Pfaff 1475CD, settings are stitch 51 W6, L2.5, Pl 10. Stitch across the full width of the skirt, making sure you leave 12 mm (½″) to 25 mm (1″) to the right of your presser foot. The fabric will pucker if stitching is too close to the raw edge.
- When you have finished the scalloping, run Fray Stoppa or similar fabric glue along outside edge of scallops. Let dry, and cut away excess fabric with small embroidery scissors as shown in diagram.
- Cut a length of fabric 38 cm (15″) long x 10 cm (4″) wide for shoulder ruffles. Give this fabric the same treatment as for skirt edge and stitch scallop embroidery on. Cut away excess fabric as for skirt edge.

Cutting away excess fabric to create scalloped edge

METHOD FOR APRON

Cut out shoulder straps and waistband as per pattern.

- Roll and whip (zigzag W3.5 L1) narrow edge lace to centre back edges of apron, right sides together. Apron is open down centre back.
- Fold back lace and press.
- Add two rows of gathering stitches at top edge of skirt.
- Pull up gathering to fit skirt to waistband, matching centre front and notches; distribute gathers evenly. Stitch together. Tidy up seam and finish off using small zigzag stitch (W2 L2).
- Cut shoulder ruffles with straight edge of pattern to scallop edge of fabric you have prepared.
- Run two rows of gathering stitches along curved edge of shoulder ruffle.
- Place between notches on shoulder straps and pull up gathers to fit, distributing gathers evenly. Stitch together along seam line and trim.
- Fold strap on fold line and press. Turn under raw edge and slip stitch underside strap to seam of shoulder ruffle.
- Place shoulder straps on waistband, matching notches on waistband, making sure you have the correct length of shoulder strap by checking apron over dress on doll before stitching shoulder straps in place.

Attaching shoulder strap to waistband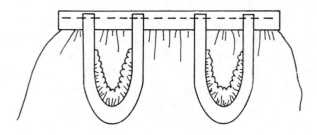

- When correct length is found, stitch straps in place on waistband.
- Make sure shoulder ruffles are right side up.
- Place waistband facing to right side of waistband, matching notches, and stitch from A to B.
- Tidy edges, clip corners, turn in and fold raw edge under, and slip stitch to waistband. Apply Fray Stoppa or similar fabric glue to any loose threads before cutting away.

- Sew stud to apron at back waistband.
- Finish your apron off with some embroidery; we have put some grub roses around the hem and on waistband, using DMC Embroidery thread in colours pink 818 and green 524.

BONNET

This is a very simple little bonnet for a 25 cm (10″) doll. Using wire, you can mould the bonnet to fit your doll's head. You may use many different types of fabrics to give you different effects. I have used batiste, as in Twirp's apron.

MATERIALS

15 cm (6″) white batiste
2.2 m (2½ yds) 12 mm (½″) edge lace
90 cm (36″) fine milliner's wire
70 cm (28″) double-sided satin ribbon
long nose pliers
wire cutters

METHOD

Using bonnet pattern, cut two bonnets.

- With scallop edge of lace toward centre of bonnet, right sides together, straight stitch lace in place on neck edge and top edge.
- At the ends of the bonnet your lace should protrude over seam allowance in order to have a small width of lace showing when turned back.
- Place bonnet lining over bonnet and stitch together on previous stitching lines on neck edge and top edge. Leave ends open.
- Turn inside out to show lace at neck and top edges and press.
- Following stitching lines on pattern, stitch to make casing for wire to be threaded through, using straight stitch L3.
- Stitch another length of edge lace on underneath of bonnet (wrong side of lace to right side of fabric) along outside stitching line of casing at top edge, stitching into head of lace with scallop edge towards outside edge, as in diagram.

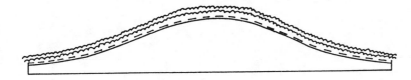

first row of lace

second row of lace

Stitching edge lace to bonnet

- Trim ends of bonnet.
- Cut lengths of wire with wire cutters, in order of length:
  top edge — 28 cm (11″)
  second top edge — 22 cm (8½″)
  middle —19 cm (7½″)
  neck edge — 18 cm (7″)
- Bend end of wire over 6 mm (¼″) to make it easier to thread wire through the casings.
- Thread all wires into casings; when they are even with the raw edge of fabric at one end, use long nose pliers to bend 6 mm (¼″) over and 6 mm (¼″) again. The ends should now be securely encased.
- Gently pull up fabric: you will need to pull up fabric on top edge and second top edge wire more than the middle and neck edge wires.
- When the wires come out the other end, be sure to have them even and then cut off bent over ends with wire cutters (being careful not to let the wires slip back into casings). Bend all wires over 6 mm (¼″) with long nose pliers and again 6 mm (¼″), so that these ends are also secured.
- Distribute ruching evenly to take shape of bonnet.
- Cut ribbon into two lengths each 35 cm (14″) long.
- Attach ribbons to sides of bonnet and embroider grub roses over ribbons, or make ribbon rosettes. We also put grub roses on inside brim of bonnet.

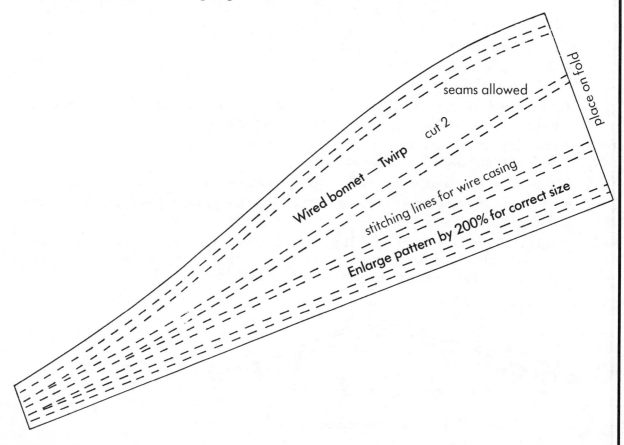

Wired bonnet — Twirp
cut 2
seams allowed
place on fold
stitching lines for wire casing
Enlarge pattern by 200% for correct size

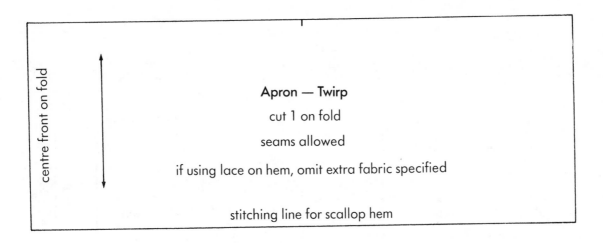

centre front on fold

Apron — Twirp

cut 1 on fold

seams allowed

if using lace on hem, omit extra fabric specified

stitching line for scallop hem

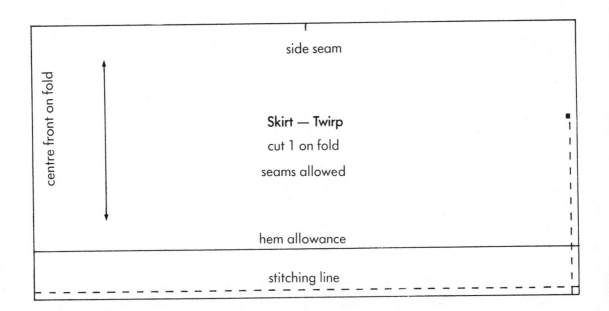

side seam

centre front on fold

Skirt — Twirp

cut 1 on fold

seams allowed

hem allowance

stitching line

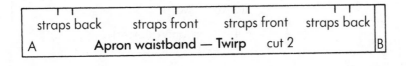

straps back   straps front   straps front   straps back

A   **Apron waistband — Twirp**   cut 2   B

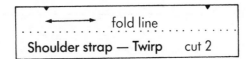

fold line

Shoulder strap — Twirp   cut 2

Enlarge patterns by 200% for correct size

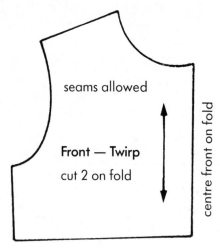

seams allowed

Front — Twirp

cut 2 on fold

centre front on fold

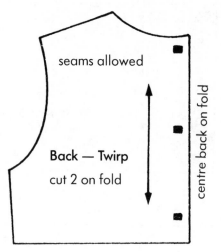

seams allowed

Back — Twirp

cut 2 on fold

centre back on fold

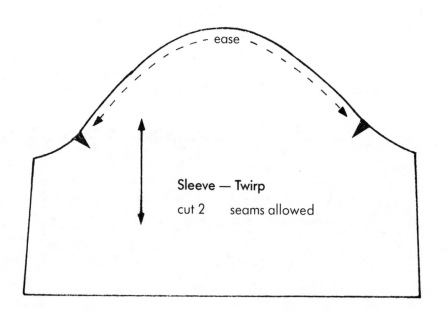

ease

Sleeve — Twirp

cut 2   seams allowed

Patterns are actual size

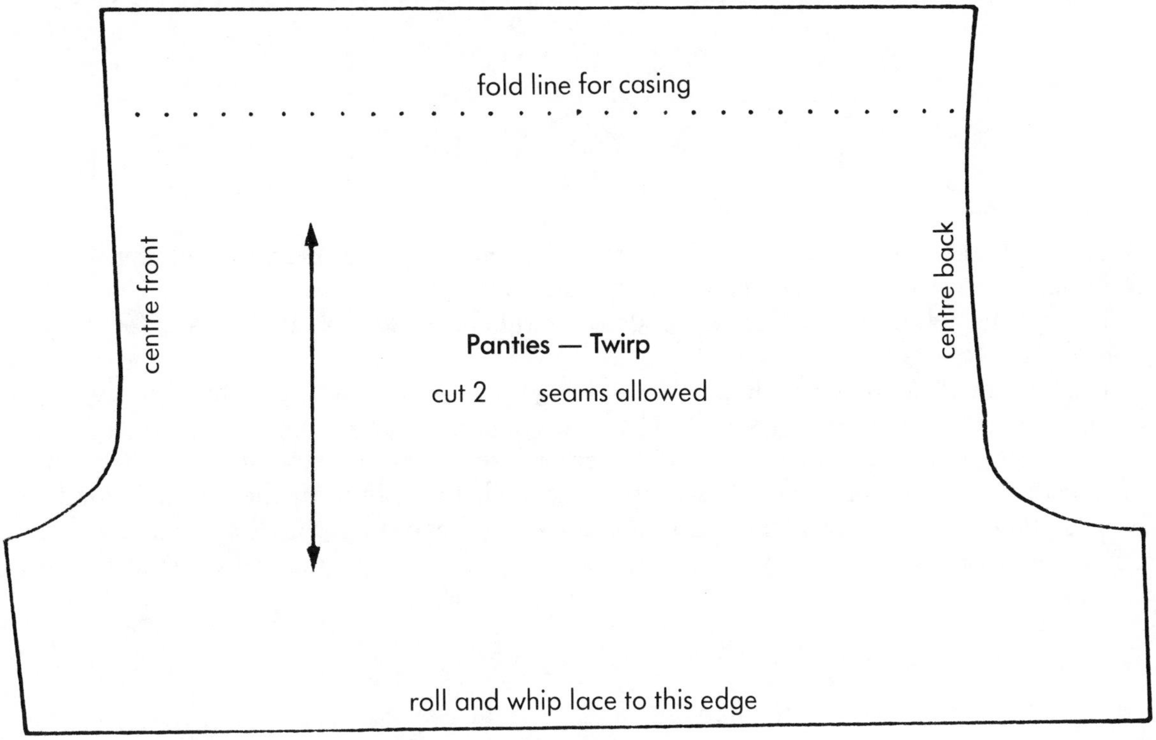

fold line for casing

centre front

centre back

Panties — Twirp

cut 2   seams allowed

roll and whip lace to this edge

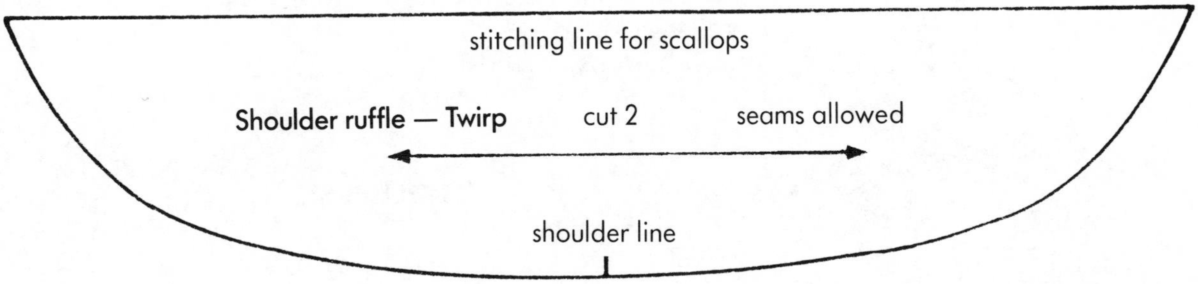

stitching line for scallops

Shoulder ruffle — Twirp   cut 2   seams allowed

shoulder line

Patterns are actual size

JOHAN
A 45 cm (18 inch) DOLL WITH A COMPOSITION BODY

Boy dolls seem to be somewhat forgotten. I think they complement a young lady: you can have a lovely pair set in a particular scene.

This young fellow we are going to dress is the beautiful Johan. He is a German doll 45 cm (18″) tall.

You just need to make a simple outfit for your young fellow and he will always be smart. Add a few accessories and it changes him altogether.

I am using a very old piece of blue tweed trouser fabric I found in my collection of fabrics (which we all have). His coat, made with box pleats in the front, is made of pale blue wool challis. His shoes and socks are handmade articles that can be purchased from doll shops or you may like to purchase commercially made shoes and socks.

MATERIALS

25 cm (10″) blue tweed fabric for trousers and beret
30 cm (12″) pale blue wool challis for coat
15 cm (6″) hat lining for beret
DMC thread — No. 4838 pale blue
small hook and eye
machine embroidery thread colour to match pale blue wool challis
blue fabric marking pen for marking pleats
pressing cloth
small buttons or studs

TROUSERS

METHOD

Cut:
  2 trouser pieces
  2 leg bands
  1 waistband

• Stitch darts together on trouser pieces down to marking on pattern. Finish off raw edges using zigzag stitch W3 L1.5. Using zigzag stitch, finish off raw edges down the front of trousers to crotch as in diagram. Use Fray Stoppa or similar fabric glue along zigzagged edge on both fronts.

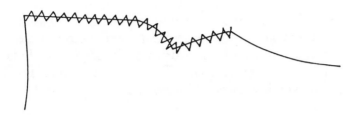

Finishing off front raw edges to crotch

- Join centre fronts together and stitch front seam from large marking on pattern to seam edge.
- Fold back fly section on fold line of right hand side. Press. Straight stitch down stitching line marked on pattern. Press.
- Place right hand side on top of left hand side and stitch from small marking to centre front seam as in diagram.

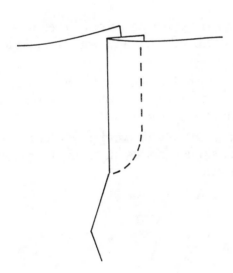

Fold back fly section and stitch

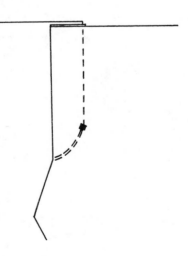

Place right side on top and stitch from small marking to centre front seam

- Join centre back seams and finish off raw edges using zigzag stitch.
- Fold tuck in place, stitch two rows of gathering threads between darts across back. Pull up to fit waistband.
- Attach waistband, matching markings on patterns. Finish raw edges off using zigzag stitch. Fold waistband on fold line and press. Turn waistband over to finish off ends as in diagram. Turn right side out. Prèss. Hand stitch waistband in place.

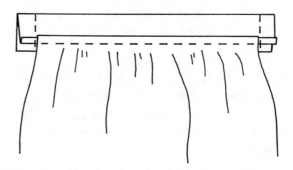

Turn waistband over to finish off ends

- Run two rows of gathering across lower legs. Pull up to fit each leg band and stitch leg band and lower leg together.
- Join leg seams, including leg band. Check the doll's leg length and calf width as doll bodies vary. Turn up leg band and hand stitch down.
- Attach hook and eye to waistband to finish off. Apply Fray Stoppa or similar fabric glue to any loose thread before cutting away.

COAT

METHOD

Cut:
    1 back
    2 fronts
    2 sleeves
    2 sleeve bands
    2 coat waistbands
    4 round collars

- Transfer markings from the front pattern to your fabric and make your box pleats, following arrows on pattern. Tack in place at the top and bottom of your pleats as in diagram.

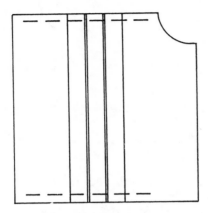

Tack box pleats in place

- Press each pleat as you make it. By using a pressing cloth, you will give a sharp fold to your pleat.
- Join front yokes to pleated fronts and trim seam. Press seam towards yoke and top stitch across yoke on right side as in diagram. Repeat on other front.

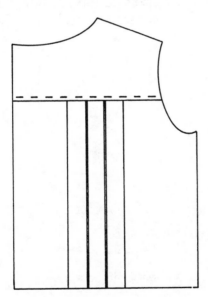

Top stitch across yoke

- Fold front facing back on fold line, then fold again, to give a neat finish on the inside. Straight stitch on both stitching lines.
- Join shoulder seams, front and back, and finish raw edges using roll and whip method or french seams.
- Join collars to collar facings.

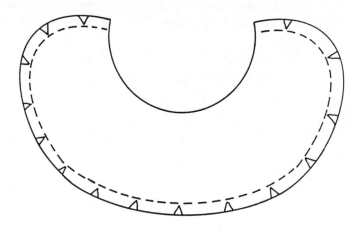

Clip into collar seam

- Stitch around stitching line of collar. Clip into seam as in diagram.
- Turn right sides out and press. At this point I have put machine embroidery around the edge of the collar. If you want to do hand embroidery, of course finish your garment first. The machine embroidery I have used is done on a Pfaff 1473 CD or 1475 CD and is stitch 48 W4 L4. Pivot as you go around collar. A piece of greaseproof paper underneath is desirable.
- Join collar to coat at neckline; collar should sit at inside top stitching line on both front yokes. Match centre backs and stitch collar around neckline. Clip neckline as in diagram.

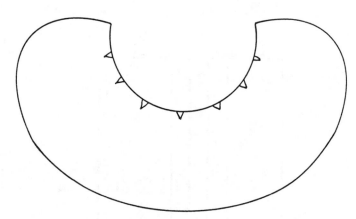

Clipping into neckline

- Cut a bias strip 25 mm (1″) longer than neck measurement and 19 mm (¾″) wide. Stitch bias strip on previous stitch line around neck, leaving 12 mm (½″) overlapping at each end. Fold ends in neatly, fold bias strip under, around the neck, and hand stitch down.
- Run two rows of gathering stitch between notches on head of each sleeve. Pull up to fit armholes. Stitch in place and finish raw edges using roll and whip method, i.e. zigzag W3.5 L1.

- Cut bias strip 9 cm (3½″) long and 12 mm (½″) wide. Slash bottom edge of sleeve to match markings on pattern. Attach bias strip along stitching line for placket on sleeve and turn bias strip in and under; stitch down. Press placket so that one side sits on the other.
- Fold tucks in place at bottom edge of sleeve and stitch in place to hold. Press.
- Join underarm seams through side seams, trim and tidy raw edges with roll and whip method or french seam.
- Attach sleeve band as in diagram.

Attaching sleeve band

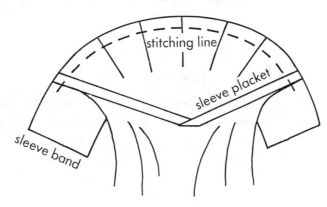

- Press on fold of sleeve band and turn band right sides together.
- Stitch down sides of sleeve band as in diagram.

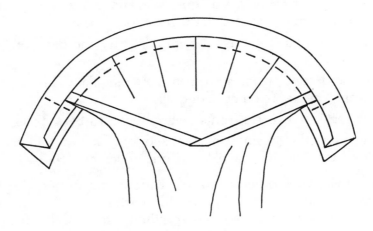

Stitch down sides of sleeve band

- Trim seams and fold right side out. Turn in hem and slip stitch in place.
- Run two rows of gathering stitches across bottom edge of back, only between notches on pattern. Pin waistband in place, overlapping each front and matching side seams to markings on pattern. Pull up gathering threads across back to fit waistband and adjust gathers evenly. Stitch waistband to coat. Trim seam and stitch down sides of waistband as in sleeve bands.
- Turn right side out, turn hem in and slip stitch down. Apply Fray Stoppa or similar fabric glue to any loose threads before cutting away.
- Make buttonholes (either by machine or hand) down the front of coat and on sleeve bands where markings are shown on pattern (or use studs). Apply Fray Stoppa or similar fabric glue to buttonholes with a pin, let dry and cut open with embroidery scissors. If using studs, attach buttons first to right side, then attach studs on inside.

BERET

I have used the same fabric for Johan's beret as for his trousers. It is a very simple beret. Sometimes you find Johan with a peaked cap, which looks lovely as well.

METHOD

Cut:
    1 beret crown in fabric and lining
    1 beret brim in fabric and lining
    1 beret head band

- Join beret crown to beret brim, making sure you stitch exactly on your 6 mm (¼") seam line all the way around the crown. This will keep your perfect circle — otherwise you will end up with little peaks every now and again.
- Repeat for lining.
- Trim back seams and turn right side out. With the beret fabric, roll the seam flat with your finger as ironing will flatten the seam too sharply.
- Put lining inside and pin together at brim edge. Try the beret on Johan's head to make sure it fits.
- Join seam of head band, trim, and open seam out flat. This is to distribute the bulk of the seam. Check size on head of doll.
- Match centre backs and centre fronts of head band to beret brim, lining included.
- Stitch around 6 mm (¼") seam, trim seam and fold band on fold line (if you haven't already pressed the fold line in place). Turn under hem and slip stitch in place.

You may add a small covered button to the centre crown of beret, or bring the beret crown down to one side and stitch in place with button.

Remember that this beret is designed specifically for a doll with painted hair; if you want to have this beret for a wigged doll, it would have to be a smaller doll or you would have to increase the size of the pattern.

TWIRP, WEARING PRETTY HAILSPOT DRESS, WHITE APRON AND
RUCHED BONNET

DETAIL OF TWIRP'S APRON AND BONNET

JOHAN IN WOOLLEN COAT, TROUSERS AND MATCHING BERET

HILDA WEARING SMOCKED BUBBLE SUIT AND PIPED BERET

DETAIL OF JOHAN'S COMBINATION UNDERWEAR AND BERET

BACK OF HILDA'S BUBBLE SUIT WITH HILDA IN UNDERWEAR

UNDERWEAR

MATERIALS
20 cm (8″) white batiste
DMC polycotton thread — white
5 mm (¼″) buttons

METHOD
Cut:
    1 back on fold
    2 fronts
    2 pants backs
    2 pants fronts

UNDERSHIRT

- Join shoulder seams and side seams. Finish off seams using roll and whip method, i.e. zigzag W3.5 L1. Press. Turn a hem under around armhole and straight stitch down.
- Fold front facings back on fold line, press, turn under small hem at raw edge and press again. Pin in place and straight stitch on right side to give a neat finish.
- Turn under hem around neck line and straight stitch down. Repeat around bottom edge of shirt.
- Make buttonholes (either by machine or hand) to match markings on pattern. Apply Fray Stoppa or similar fabric glue to buttonholes with a pin, let dry and cut open with embroidery scissors.
- Sew on small buttons.

PANTS

- Join fronts at seam line, stitching from small marking on pattern down to crotch.
- Fold fabric along fold line and press, fold again and press again. Stitch down front on stitching lines.
- Finish off raw edge of left side with zigzag stitch.
- Clip into seam where marked.
- Place right hand side of front over left hand side of front, as in diagram.

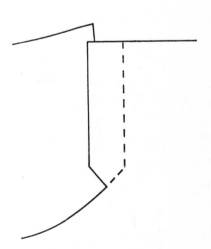

Form V-shape at seam ending

- Stitch on previous stitch lines to give you a 'V' shape as in diagram.

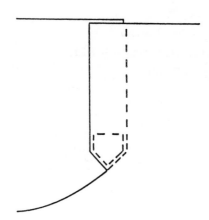

Stitch on previous stitch lines to give V-shape

- Join centre back seam and then join front to back at side seams. Finish off seams with roll and whip method (zigzag W3.5 L1). Turn up hem around legs and straight stitch around.

- Making sure that the front fly matches on both sides, turn under waist hem and straight stitch around. Apply Fray Stoppa or similar fabric glue to any loose ends before cutting away.

- Make buttonhole (by machine or hand) and apply Fray Stoppa or similar fabric glue to buttonhole with a pin, let dry and cut open with embroidery scissors.

- Sew on small button.

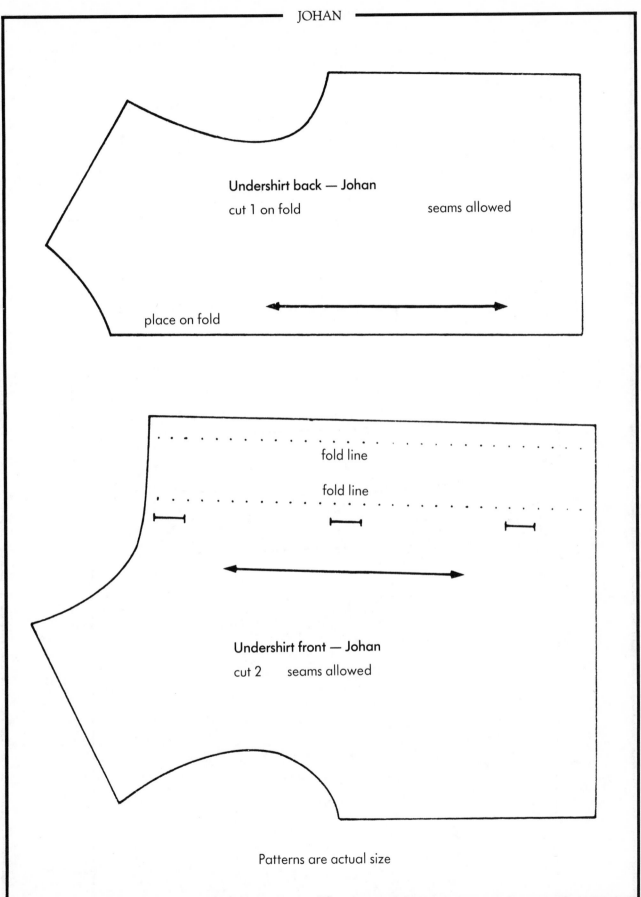

Undershirt back — Johan

cut 1 on fold   seams allowed

place on fold

fold line

fold line

Undershirt front — Johan

cut 2   seams allowed

Patterns are actual size

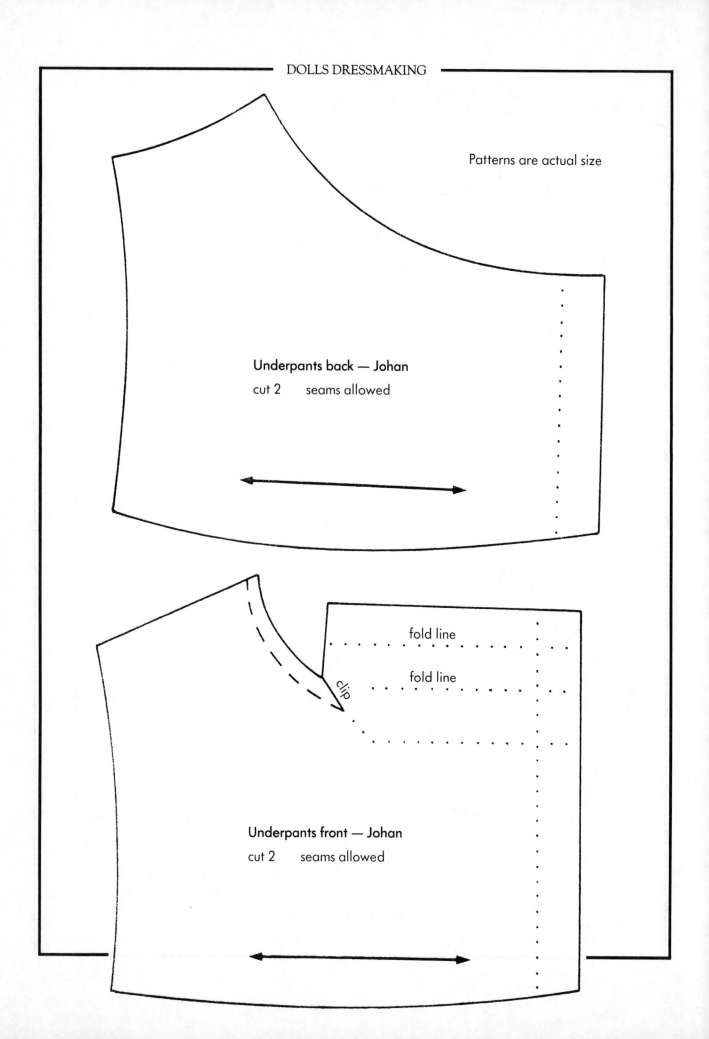

Patterns are actual size

Underpants back — Johan

cut 2   seams allowed

clip

fold line

fold line

Underpants front — Johan

cut 2   seams allowed

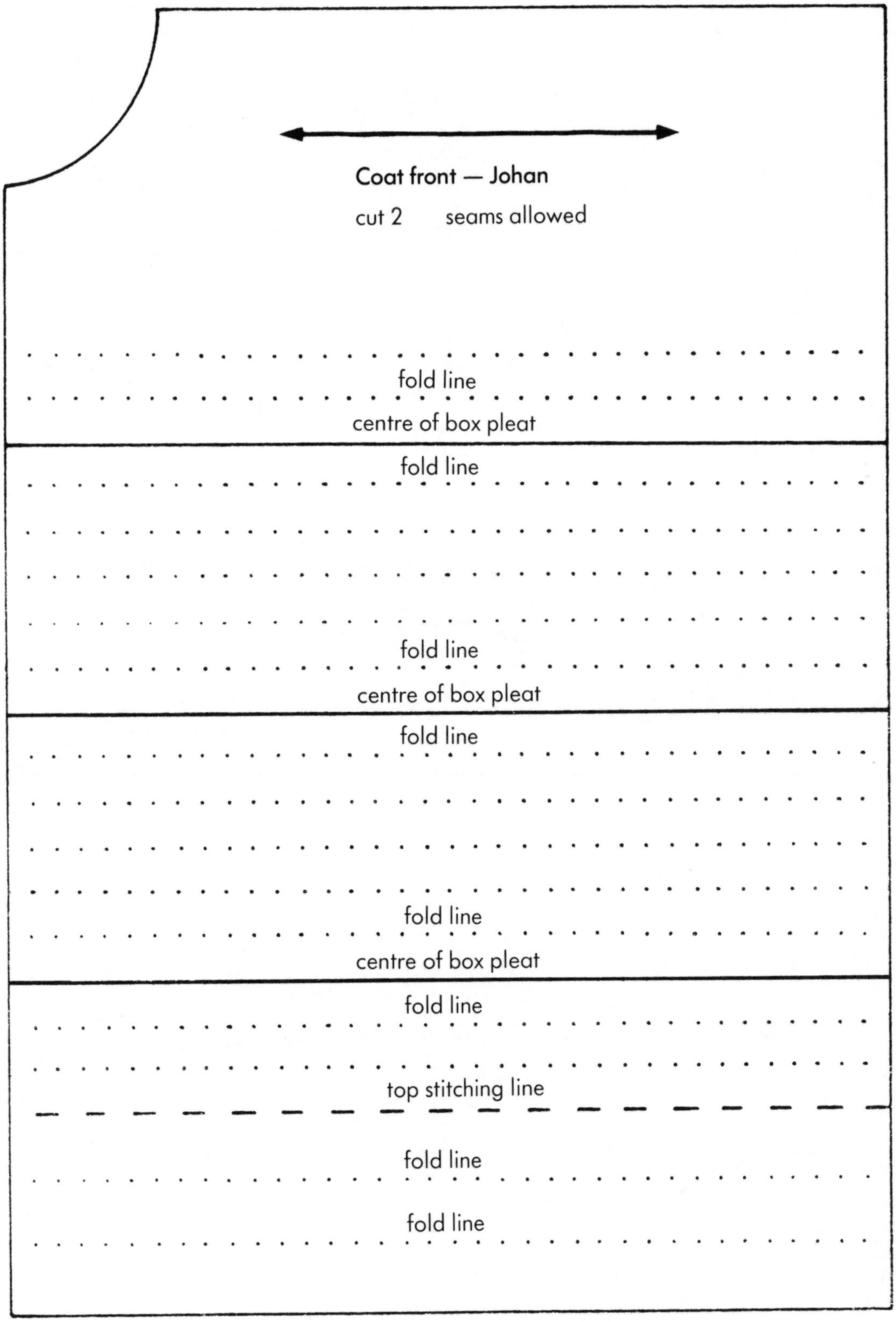

Coat front — Johan

cut 2   seams allowed

fold line

centre of box pleat

fold line

fold line

centre of box pleat

fold line

fold line

centre of box pleat

fold line

top stitching line

fold line

fold line

Pattern is actual size

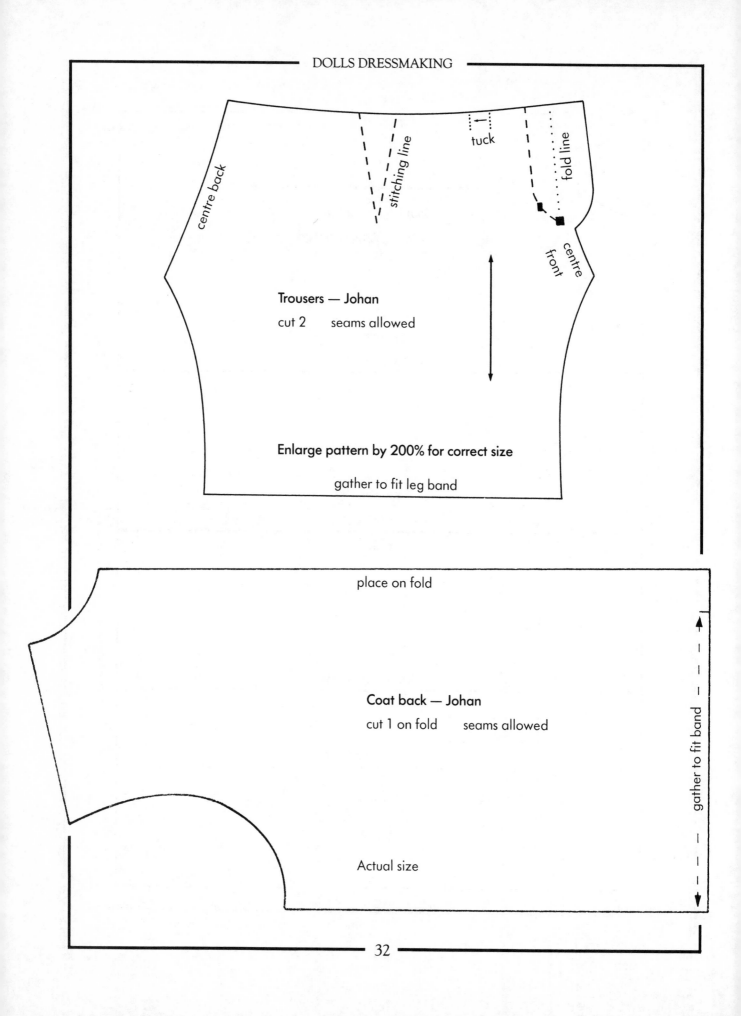

centre back

stitching line

tuck

fold line

centre front

Trousers — Johan

cut 2   seams allowed

Enlarge pattern by 200% for correct size

gather to fit leg band

place on fold

Coat back — Johan

cut 1 on fold   seams allowed

gather to fit band

Actual size

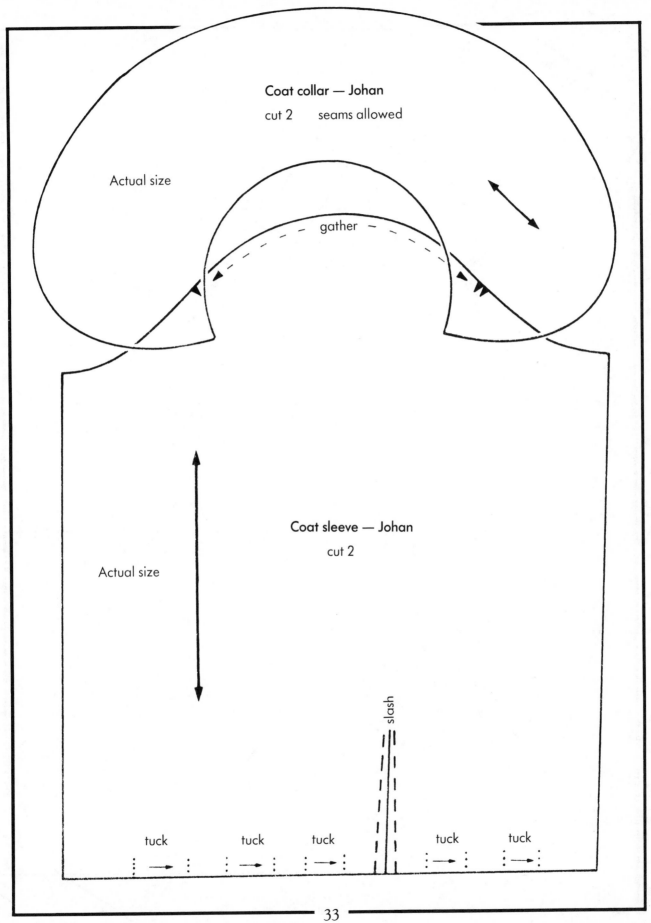

Coat collar — Johan
cut 2   seams allowed

Actual size

gather

Coat sleeve — Johan
cut 2

Actual size

slash

tuck   tuck   tuck   tuck   tuck

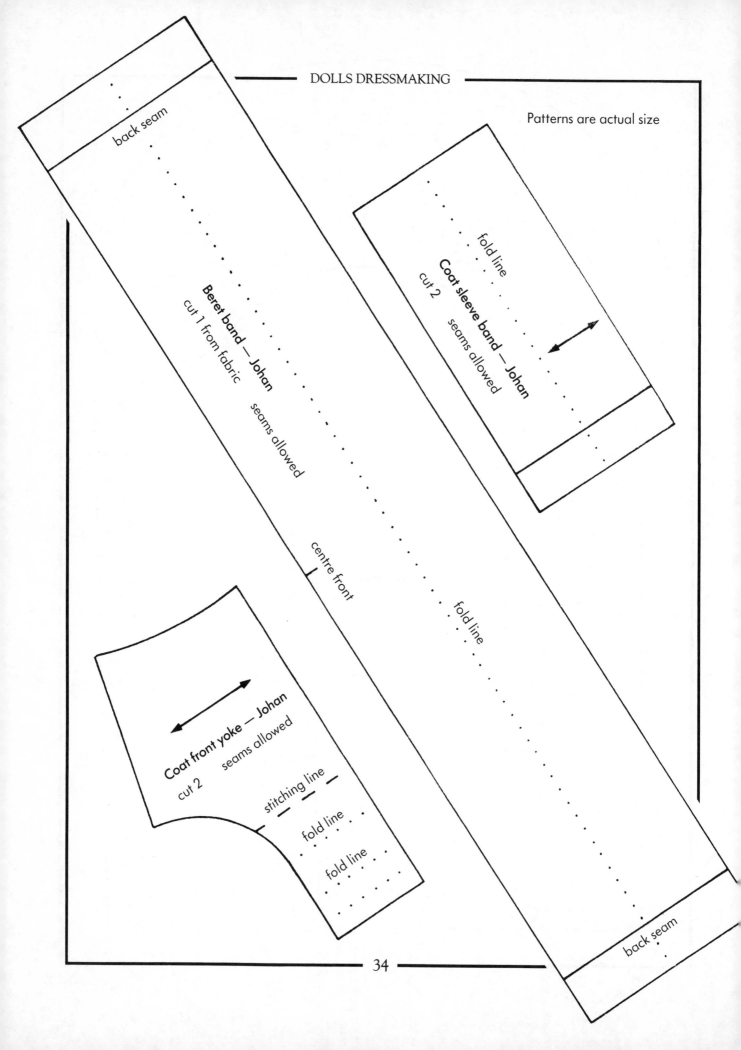

Patterns are actual size

back seam

Beret band — Johan
cut 1 from fabric

seams allowed

centre front

fold line

Coat sleeve band — Johan
cut 2

fold line

seams allowed

Coat front yoke — Johan
cut 2

seams allowed

stitching line

fold line

fold line

back seam

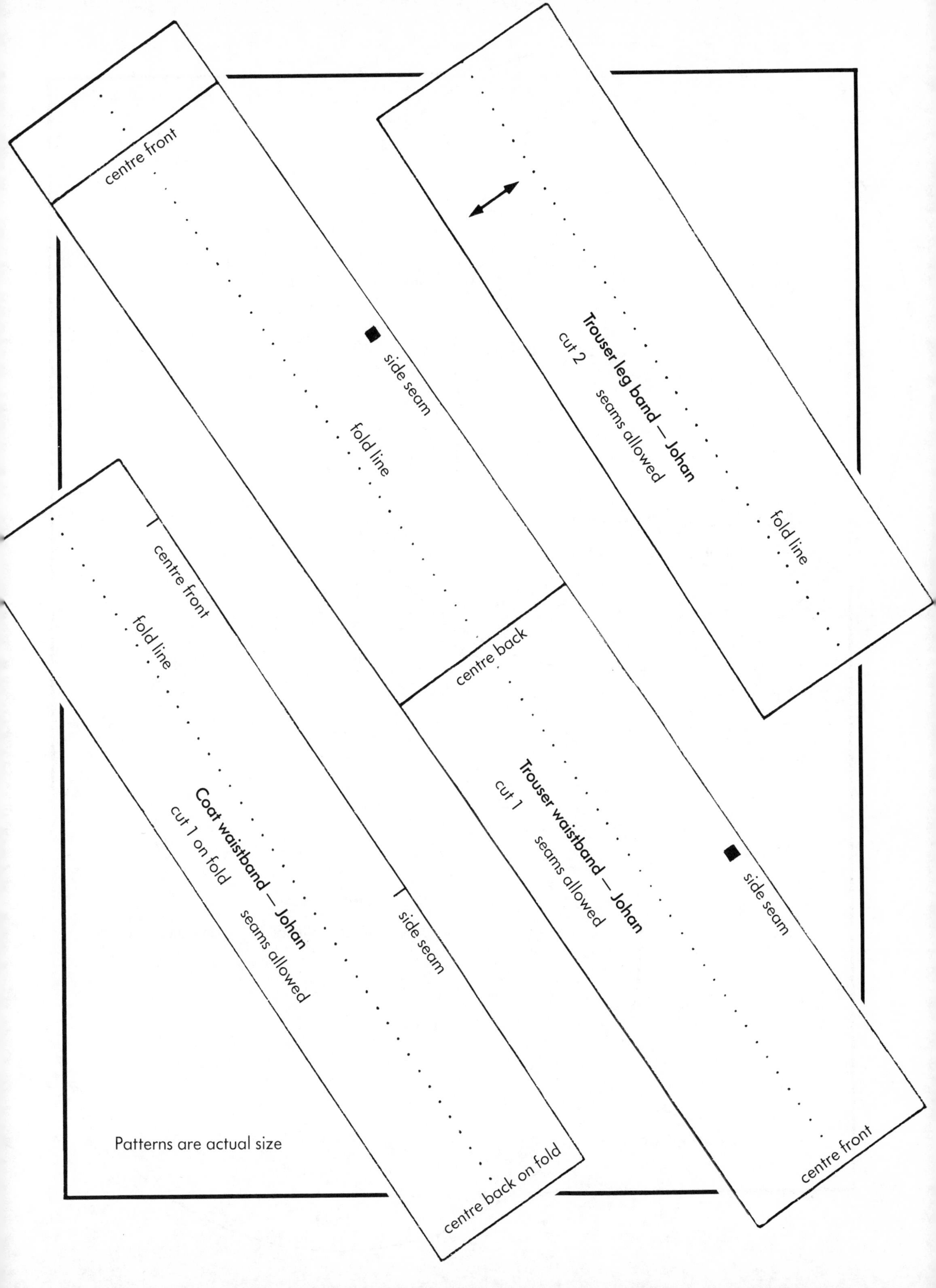

centre front

Trouser leg band — Johan
cut 2
seams allowed

fold line

side seam

fold line

centre back

centre front

fold line

Coat waistband — Johan
cut 1 on fold
seams allowed

side seam

Trouser waistband — Johan
cut 1
seams allowed

side seam

Patterns are actual size

centre back on fold

centre front

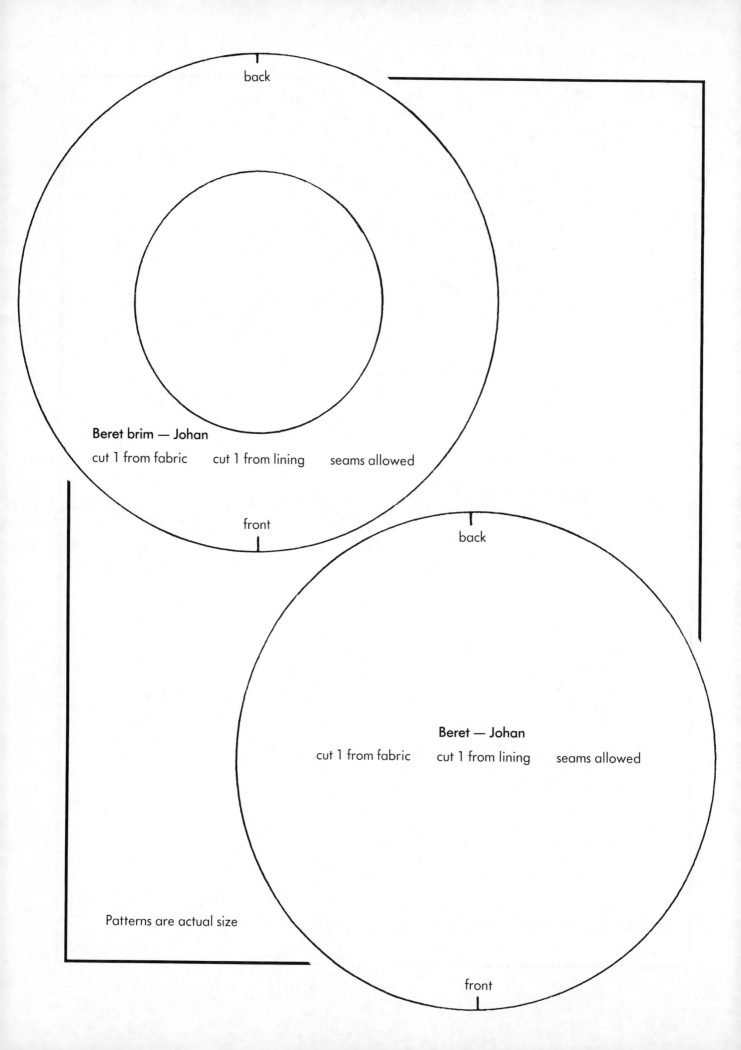

back

Beret brim — Johan

cut 1 from fabric   cut 1 from lining   seams allowed

front

back

Beret — Johan

cut 1 from fabric   cut 1 from lining   seams allowed

Patterns are actual size

front

HILDA
A 40 cm (16 inch) DOLL WITH A COMPOSITION BODY

This smocked bubble suit is made for a 40 cm (16″) Hilda. I have used white batiste and pale blue petite piping on his suit and beret. The smocking is done in two shades of DMC embroidery thread. My friend Wendy Strickland has given the suit a superb finish with her smocking. Hilda's knitted socks are available at most doll shops.

MATERIALS

70 cm (28″) white batiste
pale blue petite piping — colour 509
5 white shank buttons
DMC cotton broder thread size 50 — white
DMC embroidery thread — colours 799 and 800 blue

METHOD

Using patterns supplied, cut:
   2 front yokes
   2 back yokes on fold
   2 sleeves
   2 sleeve bands
   4 collars
   1 back waistband
   2 leg bands
   1 front pants section on fold
   1 back pants section on fold

Spray starch and press your fabric.
Use piping foot or zipper foot to attach piping.

SMOCKING DESIGN

- Pleat 9 half rows, allowing holding rows top and bottom.
- Centre design. Design is smocked using two strands of DMC thread.

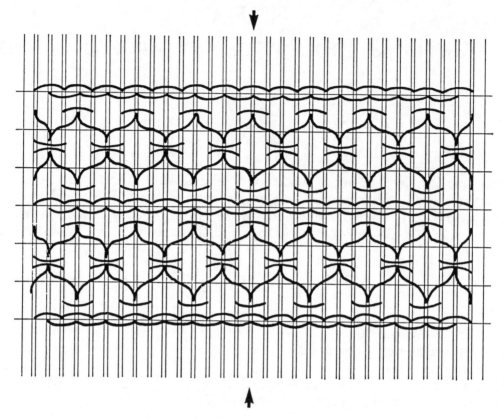

Smocking design

Row 1   Cable stitch in DMC 799
Row 1¼   Baby wave in DMC 800 over ½ row
Row 1¾   Baby wave in DMC 800 over ½ row to form a diamond with row 1¼
Row 2½   Cable stitch in DMC 799
Row 2¾   Baby wave in DMC 800 over ½ row
Row 3¼   Baby wave in DMC 800 over ½ row to form a diamond with row 2¾
Row 4   Cable stitch in DMC 799

BODICE

- Join shoulder seams of front and back yokes. Finish seams using roll and whip method (zigzag W3.5 L1). Press back bodices on fold line.
- Clip piping to make it easier to attach to collars.
- Stitch piping around two collars, raw edges to raw edges. You will find it easier if you put two layers of greaseproof paper under the collars.
- When you have attached piping to collars, place collar facings right side to right side on these collars using previous stitching line and stitch together (still using piping or zipper foot and greaseproof paper).

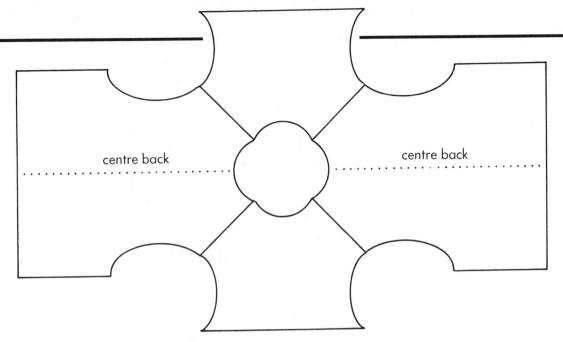

Joining shoulder seams of front and back yokes

- Trim seam and clip around collar. Turn to right side and press.
- Find centre front of front yoke and mark; mark collar line on back bodice, and pin collars in place around neckline. Collars must butt together at centre front.
- When in place, stitch around neckline from centre back through to centre back, keeping facings free.
- Bring facings over and match shoulder seams and centre front. Stitch around neckline on previous stitching line. Clip and turn right side out and press.
- Stitch piping across right side of front yoke on seam line, keeping facing free. Now you are ready to attach your smocked front section.
- Using smocking plate provided, or your own design, smock front section, making sure your smocked front section fits your front yoke. When finished, join to front yoke, making sure you keep your piping close to your cable for a neat finish.
- Bring back facing to back bodice, right sides together, and stitch across bottom edge of back bodice on 6 mm (¼″) seam line.
- Trim seam, turn right sides out and press.
- Pin facing to front yoke and slip stitch across front, enclosing seam.
- Match shoulder seams of bodice and facing, and pin.
- Stitch two rows of gathering stitches at sleeve edges.
- Stitch piping to one edge of sleeve band, pin sleeve edge to piped edge of sleeve band, pull up gathering to fit sleeve band, distribute gathers evenly, and stitch together on previous stitching line. Repeat for other sleeve.
- Stitch two rows of gathering stitches between notches on sleeve head.
- Pin sleeve to armhole, matching sleeve head to shoulder seam and underarm notches, pull up gathering to fit, distributing gathers evenly.
- Stitch sleeves in place through facings as well. Trim armhole seams and finish off using roll and whip method (zigzag W3.5 L1).

BACK OF SUIT

- Press waistband on fold line.
- Stitch two rows of gathering stitches along top of pants back between notches. Pull up to fit back waistband, matching notches on waistband to back pants, and distribute gathers evenly.
- With raw edges together, stitch in place between notches. Trim seam.
- Fold waistband right sides together and stitch down right sides of waistband, keeping pants free, as in diagram.

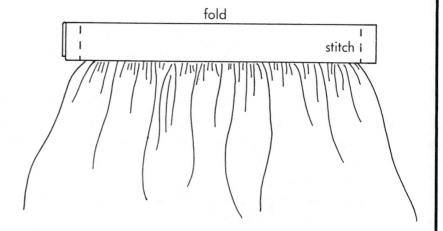

Stitch down sides of waistband

- Trim seam, turn right side out, turn up hem and slip stitch waistband together along seam. Press.
- Match back section to front at side seams and stitch together, keeping waistband free.
- Match back bodice to side seam and underarm sleeve seam. Back bodice must be placed over back pant section, otherwise back opening will not work.
- Stitch side seams from edge of sleeve cuff through to back bodice, always keeping waistband free. Trim seam and finish off. Repeat for other side seam.
- Turn in sleeve bands on fold line, turn up hems and slip stitch into place.
- Stitch two rows of gathering stitches around leg openings.
- Stitch piping to one side of leg band as for sleeve band.
- Pin leg band to leg opening and pull up gathering

to fit, distributing gathers evenly, and stitch together on previous stitching line. Repeat for other leg band.

- Join crotch seam through leg bands as well. Trim seams and finish off.

- Turn leg bands in on fold lines, turn up hems and slip stitch into place.

- Make buttonholes by machine or hand. Run Fray Stoppa or similar fabric glue down centre of buttonhole with a pin, let dry and cut with embroidery scissors.

- You will be making three buttonholes down back bodice, and three across back waistband. The middle buttonhole on waistband will go over button with lower bodice buttonhole, as in diagram.

- Attach buttons.

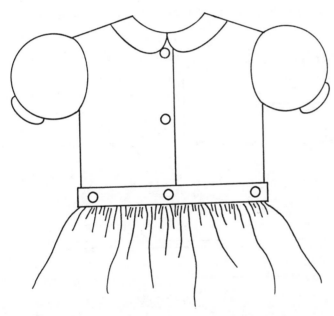

Lower bodice button also goes through middle buttonhole on waistband

BERET

Using patterns supplied, cut:
    2 beret crowns
    2 beret brims
    1 beret band

- Clip piping for length of outside beret crown.

- Stitch piping around outside edge of one beret crown, raw edges together. Start stitching piping 25 mm (1″) from start of piping; stitch around to within 25 mm (1″) of start. *Do not cut* piping off yet.

- Unpick stitches on the piping you have left free at the beginning back to where you started machine stitching; cut away rope only to where machine stitching starts. Fold bias to inside 12 mm (½″) and press.

- Place piping strip that you have not cut so that it sits firmly in place inside the other bias strip. Cut piping where it butts to other end of piping.

- Bring bias fabric down over piping and stitch over section that you had left unstitched, as in diagrams, and press.

- Stitch one beret brim to crown over previous stitching. Trim seam and clip as in diagram.

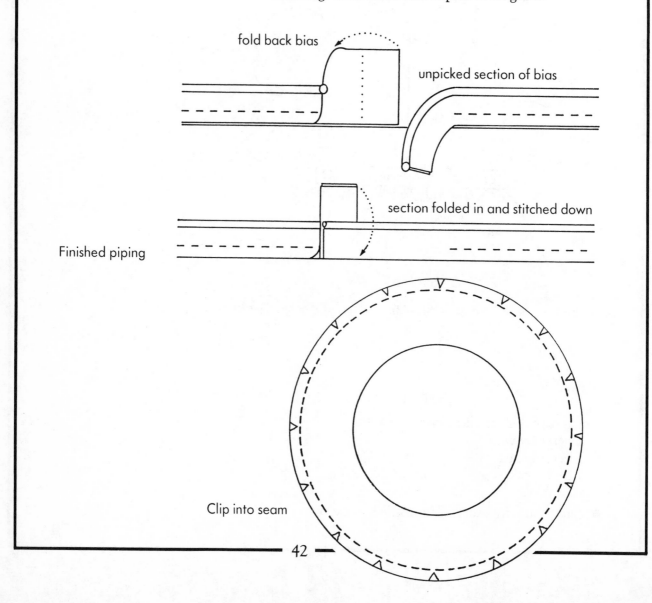

fold back bias

unpicked section of bias

section folded in and stitched down

Finished piping

Clip into seam

CAMILLE IN PINK WOOL CHALLIS FULL-SKIRTED DRESS AND
TAFFETA-LINED CAPE

CAMILLE'S PETTICOAT AND PANTALOONS AND CAPE SHOWING SOFT
TAFFETA LINING

SLEEPING JENNY IN CHRISTENING LAYETTE EMBELLISHED WITH LACE
AND EMBROIDERY

DETAIL OF CHRISTENING DRESS AND BONNET

DETAIL OF UNDERWEAR, CROCHETED SHOES AND BOOTIES,
PETTICOAT AND BONNET FOR CHRISTENING LAYETTE

- Turn right side out and press.
- Stitch remaining crown to brim and trim seam. Clip as in diagram and press.
- Place beret lining inside beret, matching centre backs and centre fronts.
- Raw edges together, stitch 3 mm (⅛″) from raw edge all the way around opening; this will hold beret and lining together while you attach beret band.
- Stitch piping on to beret band on 6 mm (¼″) seam line.
- Check band length around head, join side seams and press open.
- Fold band in half on fold line and press, matching back seam on band to centre back on beret and matching fronts.
- Stitch band and beret together. Piping should now be against brim of beret.
- Turn up band and turn in hem. Slip stitch band in place on seam line.
- Make tassel from DMC embroidery thread colour 800 and attach to centre of beret crown.

UNDERWEAR

This set of underwear is so easy to make you will be thrilled with yourself. It is made from stretch fabric called Rib Trim and gives less bulk to the outfit.

MATERIALS

30 cm (12″) Rib Trim fabric
40 cm (16″) 10 mm (⅖″) stretch lace
DMC polycotton thread — white
Stretch needle size 75

METHOD

Using patterns supplied, cut
   1 singlet on fold
   1 underpants on fold

When cutting out your pattern in this fabric, make sure the grain of fabric is very straight. This is important to avoid a twisted look.

- Using your overlocker, set your machine to rolled hem. On my overlocker, which is a Pfaff 796, the settings are as follows:
  cutting or stitch width 3
  stitch length 1.4-1.5
  My tensions are set at:
  right needle N + 1
  top Looper + 5
  lower Looper + 2
  differential feed 0.05

You may have to adjust your own setting to suit fabric on other brands of machine. If you do not have an overlocker, you can use an overlocking stitch or a shell edge on your sewing machine to finish off edge.
  Check your machine instruction book for these procedures.

SINGLET

- Attach stretch lace around neckline, using zigzag W4 L4. Starting at shoulder, place your stretch lace on top of right side of fabric with edges together.
- Sew a few stitches and then gently stretch your lace and stitch around neckline in this manner until you are back at the beginning; overstitch and finish off.
- If necessary, trim away fabric from behind edge of stretch lace.
- Using overlocker on settings given above, stitch around armholes, then join side seams and finally stitch around bottom edge of singlet. If using sewing machine, stitch around armholes using overlocking stitch; check your machine instruction book as procedures differ for individual machines.
- Apply Fray Stoppa or similar fabric glue to any loose threads before cutting away.

UNDERPANTS

- Using overlocker on settings given for singlet, or sewing machine, stitch around leg openings and then join side seams.
- Measure stretch lace around tummy of your doll to give a nice fit when stretched. This measurement is what you will stitch around top of pants.
- Join lace piece together at ends. Place pin at halfway point and quarter points; do the same on waist of pants.

- Match pins of stretch lace to pins on pants and stitch around as for the singlet neckline. You will need to stretch the lace to fit pants a little more than singlet neckline, but do not stretch pants fabric as well.
- Apply Fray Stoppa or similar fabric glue to any loose threads before cutting away.

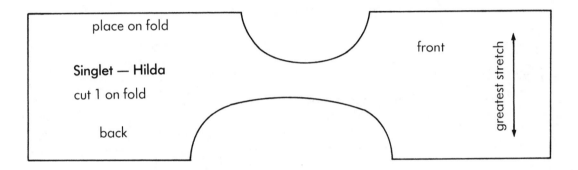

place on fold

Singlet — Hilda

cut 1 on fold

back

front

greatest stretch

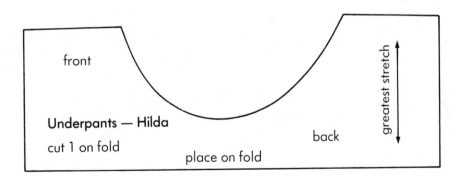

front

Underpants — Hilda

cut 1 on fold

place on fold

back

greatest stretch

Enlarge patterns by 200% for correct size

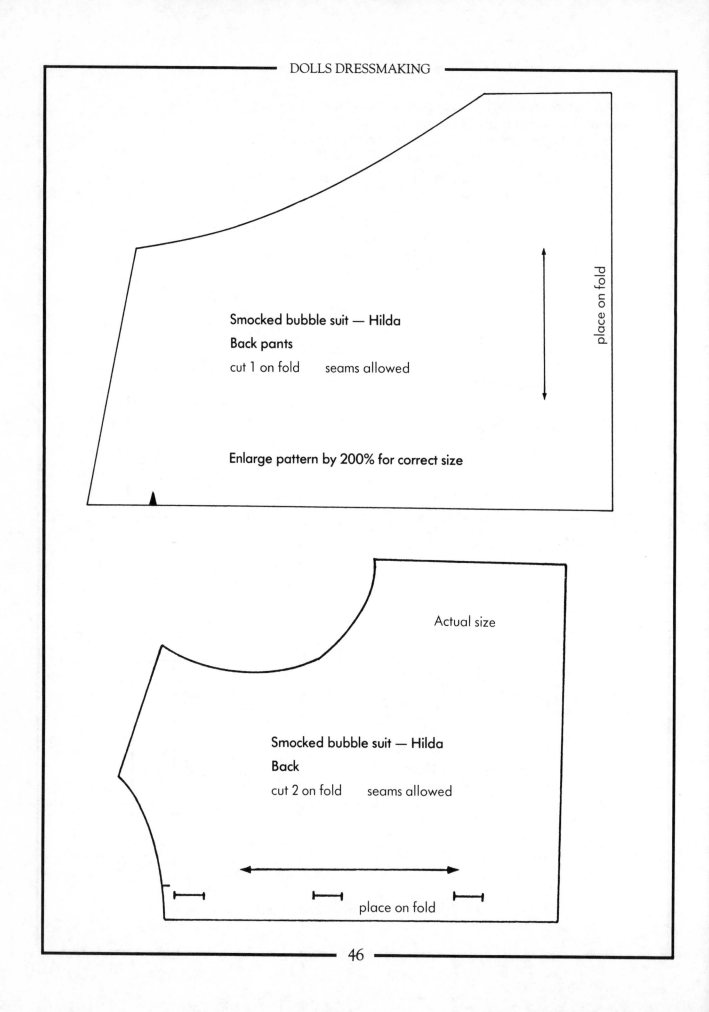

place on fold

Smocked bubble suit — Hilda

Back pants

cut 1 on fold   seams allowed

Enlarge pattern by 200% for correct size

Actual size

Smocked bubble suit — Hilda

Back

cut 2 on fold   seams allowed

place on fold

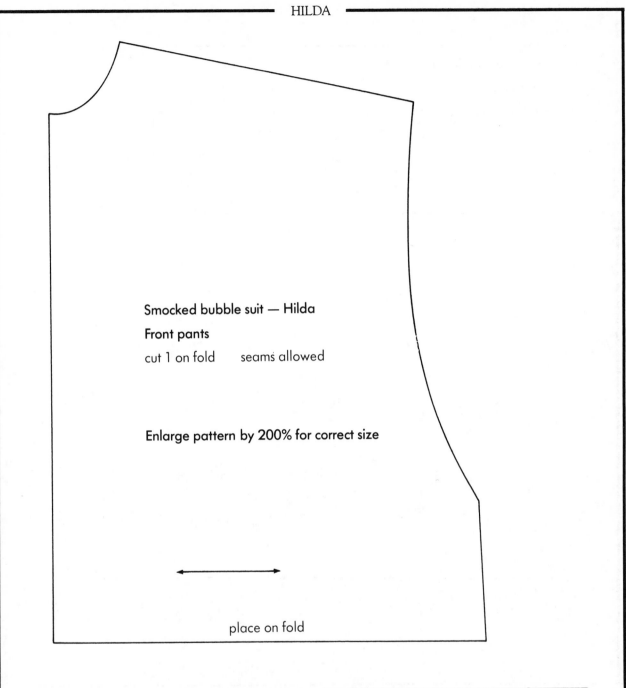

Smocked bubble suit — Hilda

Front pants

cut 1 on fold   seams allowed

Enlarge pattern by 200% for correct size

place on fold

Beret head band — Hilda

fold line

Enlarge pattern by 200% for correct size   cut 1   seams allowed

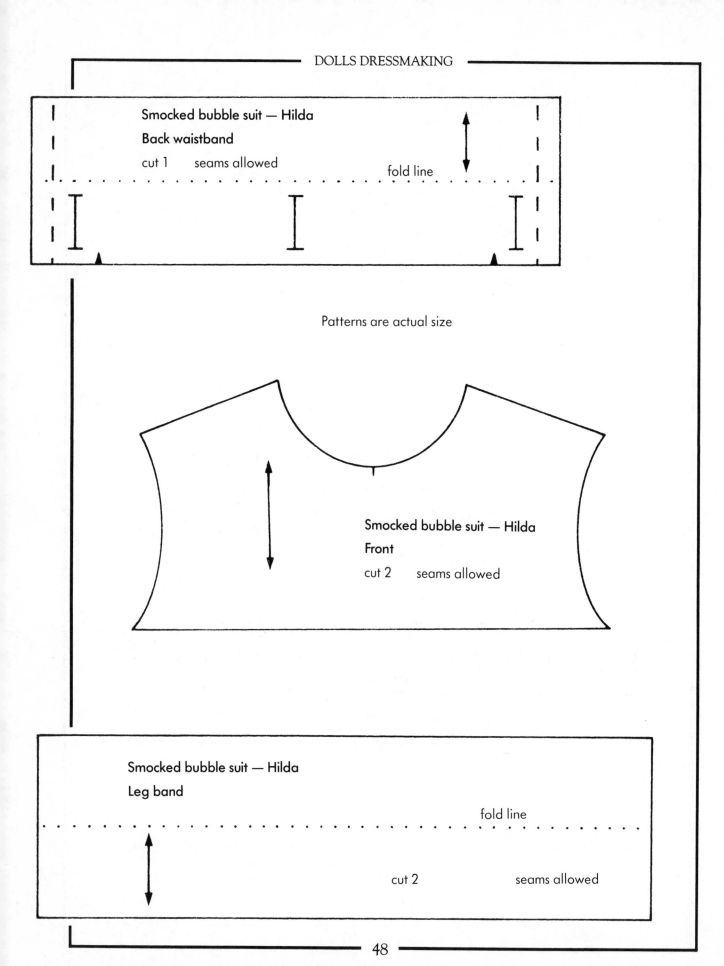

Smocked bubble suit — Hilda
Back waistband
cut 1   seams allowed
fold line

Patterns are actual size

Smocked bubble suit — Hilda
Front
cut 2   seams allowed

Smocked bubble suit — Hilda
Leg band
fold line
cut 2   seams allowed

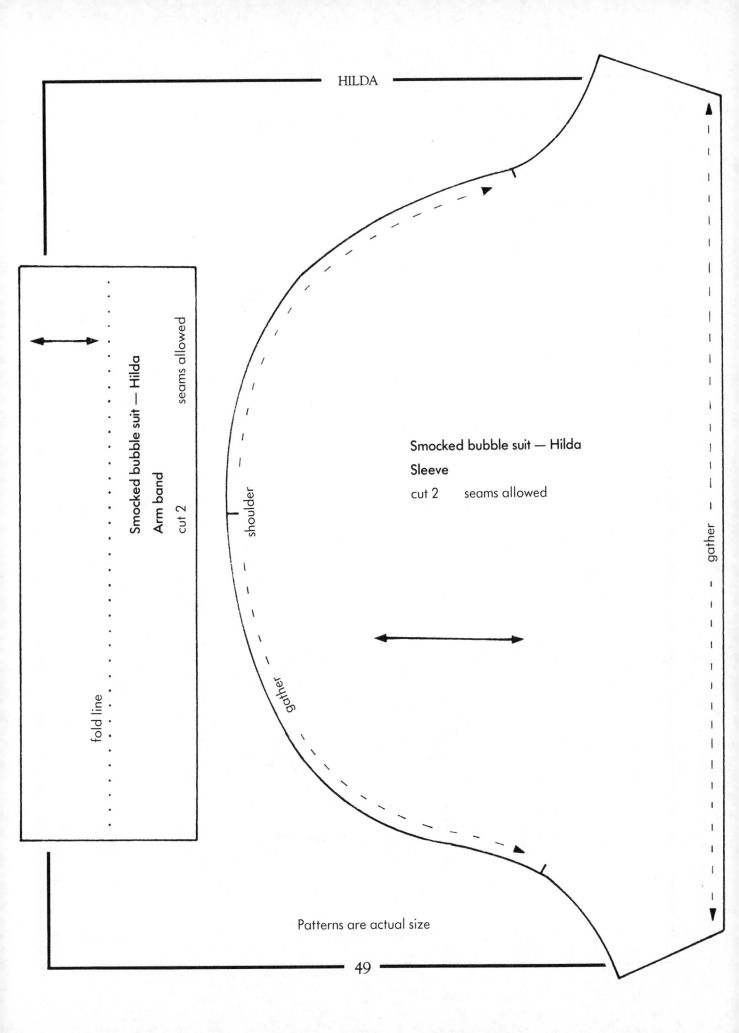

Smocked bubble suit — Hilda
Arm band
cut 2

seams allowed

fold line

shoulder

gather

Smocked bubble suit — Hilda
Sleeve
cut 2   seams allowed

gather

Patterns are actual size

Patterns are actual size

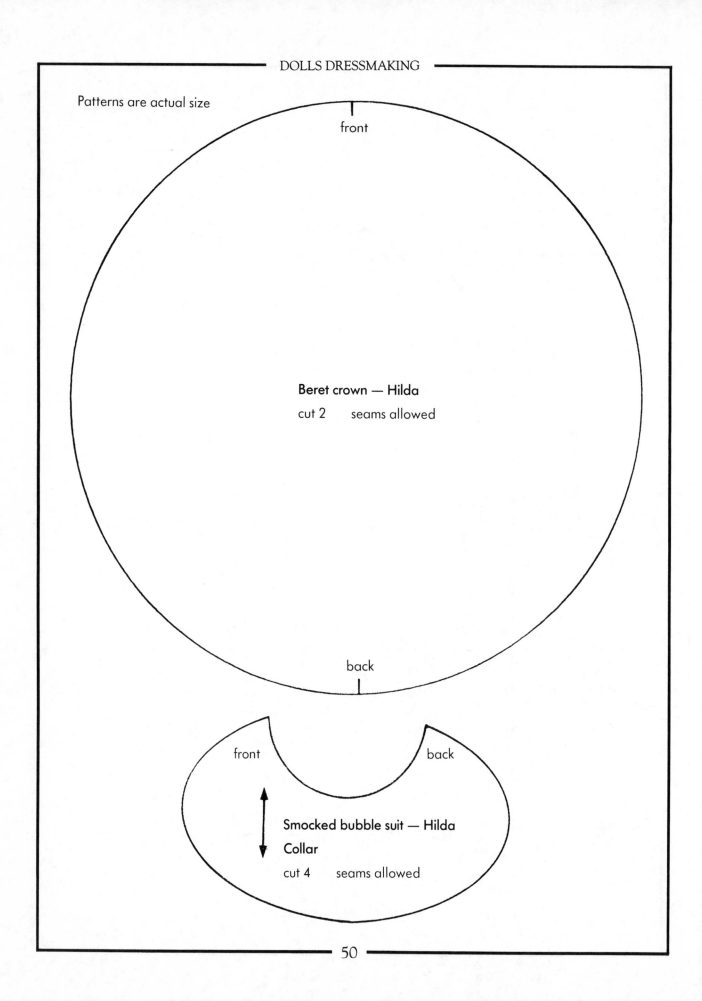

front

Beret crown — Hilda

cut 2   seams allowed

back

front   back

Smocked bubble suit — Hilda

Collar

cut 4   seams allowed

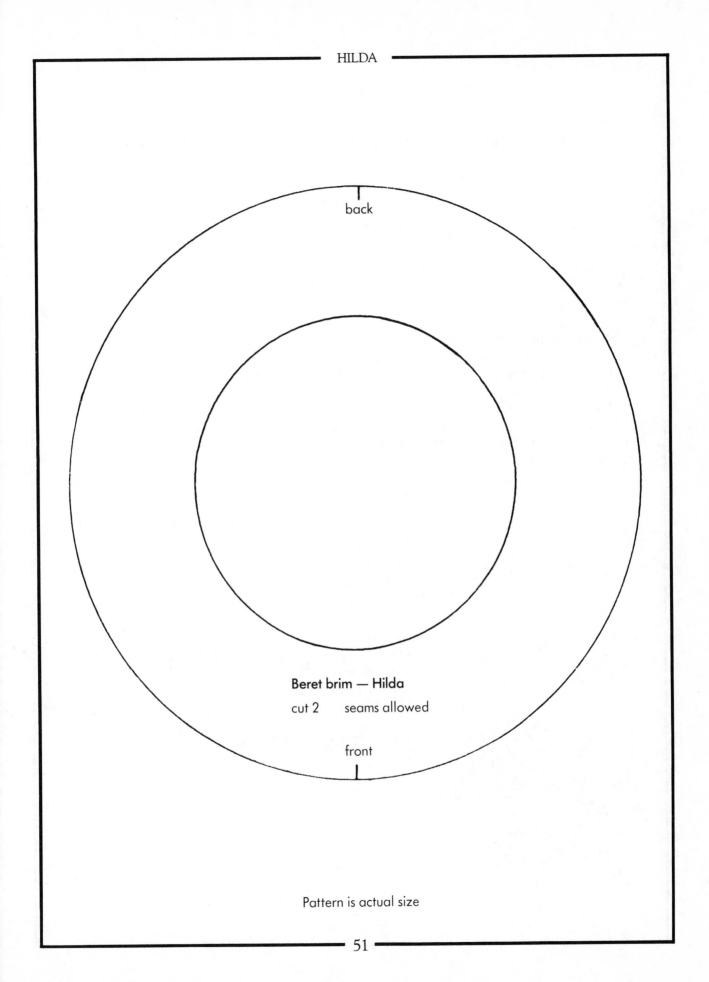

back

Beret brim — Hilda

cut 2   seams allowed

front

Pattern is actual size

CAMILLE
A 63 cm (25 inch) DOLL WITH A SOFT BODY

Camille is a beautiful young girl, sculpted by Jennifer Esteban of Australia.
I selected a doll by Jennifer because her work is very original and always reminds me of a little girl for whom I had a great affection.

I have chosen pink wool challis for Camille's outfit as it falls beautifully in the folds in the skirt and the full sleeve is beautifully gathered. Camille has a beautiful cape to keep her shoulders warm. Her cape is very simple and is lined in a soft taffeta lining. Her underwear is batiste with a lovely ecru lace to finish off the pantaloons and skirt of the petticoat. Her shoes and socks are available at most doll shops.

I hope you have as much fun dressing your Camille as I have. You can use this pattern for any 63 cm (25 inch) doll, but remember you may have to adjust your pattern measurements for chest and waist.

By using a soft fabric you will achieve a lovely fall to the shirt.

MATERIALS

1 m (40″) pink batiste for petticoat and pantaloons
2 m (2¼ yds) pink wool challis for dress and cape
70 cm (28″) taffeta lining for cape
66 cm (26″) entredeux
6 m (6½ yds) 18 mm (¾″) ecru wide edge lace
78 cm (30″) 10 mm (²⁄₅″) narrow edge lace
8.5 m (9½ yds) 12 mm (½″) ecru lace insertion
machine embroidery thread
    DMC polycotton No. 4442 to match pink batiste
    and No. 4446 to match pink wool challis
    DMC broder cotton size 50 — ecru
3 m (3¼ yds) ribbon — rose
4 x 7 mm (¼″) buttons
3 mm (⅛″) flat elastic
3 m (3¼ yds) round cord (silky) — rose

PETTICOAT AND PANTALOONS

Using the pattern in this book, cut:
  1 front bodice on fold
  2 back bodices
  1 front skirt on fold
  2 back skirts
  2 pantaloons
  Always use DMC broder cotton (size 50 ecru) to
put laces together.

METHOD FOR PANTALOONS

- Using french seams or your overlocker, join front and back seams. Press. Turn under casing on fold line; press. Make small hem in casing and straight stitch around casing, leaving an opening to thread elastic through. Straight stitch around top edge of casing as this gives a firmer casing so your pantaloons won't roll over at the top. Measure your doll's waist, as all cloth bodies differ in size (no one fills cloth bodies the same). Using this measurement, cut your elastic length and thread through casing and join together.

- Spray starch and press your laces. Cut two lengths of insertion lace 19 cm (7½″) long. Place lace on stitching line of pantaloons at bottom edge of legs. Straight stitch into head of lace. Press excess fabric back from lace, on right side. Zigzag (W1 L1) over head of lace, making sure one stitch goes into fabric and the next stitch goes into lace. Cut away excess fabric close to zigzag stitches, being careful not to cut fabric. Duck-billed scissors are good for this procedure.

- Cut two lengths of entredeux 19 cm (7½″) long. Spray starch and press. Cut fabric from one side of entredeux and butt entredeux to insertion lace, using zigzag W2 L1. Trim other side of fabric from entredeux. Press.

- Cut two lengths of edge lace 19 cm (7½″) and butt to entredeux, zigzag (W2 L1) together and press.

- Join leg seams through crotch, making sure your lace section matches perfectly. You may like to thread ribbon through entredeux to gather legs of pantaloons in to fit.

METHOD FOR PETTICOAT

- Using french seams or overlocker, join shoulder seams of front bodice to back bodices. Trim away seam allowance from armholes and neckline. Press.

- Cut narrow (10 mm/²/₅″) edge lace into two lengths of 24 cm (9½″) and one length of 30 cm (12″).

- Using roll and whip method (zigzag W3 L5), place 30 cm (12″) length of lace just inside raw edge of neckline, right sides together. Roll and whip lace to fabric around neckline, and repeat same method around armholes.

- Press centre backs on foldline to form back facing. Straight stitch down stitching line. Do not stitch into lace at top of facing, as this will stay in place when pressed.

- Join side seams. Apply Fray Stoppa or similar fabric glue to loose threads on armhole seams. Press bodice.

- Join skirt side seams.

- Cut a length of insertion lace 2.3 m (2½ yds). Spray starch and press. Place insertion lace 6 mm (¼") on outer stitching line of bottom of skirt, and straight stitch into head of lace.

- Press fabric away from lace on wrong side of skirt. Using a small zigzag (W1 L1), stitch over head of lace making sure one stitch goes into fabric and the next stitch into lace. Press and cut away excess fabric with duck bill scissors.

- Cut another length of insertion lace 2.1 m (2¼ yds). Spray starch and press. Place this insertion piece on stitching line marked on pattern 25 mm (1") from bottom row of insertion. Stitch on outer stitching line first, press, then stitch on other stitching line and press. Turn to wrong side of skirt, slash fabric down centre of stitching lines. Do not cut lace. Press excess fabric away from lace on both sides. It is easier to do one side at a time. Be careful not to stretch fabric, as it is cut on bias.

- Using zigzag W1 L1, repeat as for bottom row of insertion. Press again. The trick to making your garments neat and with a lovely finish is to press as you go.

- Run two rows of gathering stitches around waistline of skirt. Matching side seams and backs, pin skirt to bodice right side to right side. At centre backs, pin back yoke in place and fold seam allowance back around back yoke as in diagram.

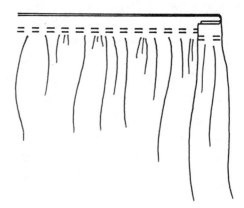

Fold seam allowance back to form facing

- Pull up fabric to fit bodice, distributing gathers evenly. Stitch in place. Trim seam and tidy with zigzag or overlocker. Check length of petticoat: try on your doll before you put the edge lace on to insertion.

- Cut a 3.5 m (3⅘ yd) length of 18 mm (¾") edge lace. Spray starch and press. Pulling the passive thread in the head of edge lace at one end, start to gather your lace, being very careful not to break your passive thread. This length of lace will give a slight gather to the bottom edge of petticoat skirt. Pull lace up to fit insertion lace and butt together using zigzag W2.5 L1.

- Finish off edges of back seam through lace as well. Stitch from markings on pattern, making sure your insertion laces match when stitching your seam. Press open.

- Make buttonholes (either by machine or hand) at markings on pattern. Run Fray Stoppa or similar fabric glue down buttonhole with a pin to prevent fraying. Sew buttons on.
- You may like to do some embroidery on your doll's underwear.

DRESS

Using your patterns and following instructions, now cut skirt without side seams. Cut:
    1 front bodice on fold
    2 back bodices on fold
    2 sleeves
    1 full circle skirt
    1 piece of fabric 35.5 cm x 19 cm (14″ x 7½″)
This is to make tucks and do lace work before cutting out bodice front.

- Prepare your 35.5 cm x 19 cm (14″ x 7½″) piece of fabric: press down centre front line and down tuck fold lines. Using a pressing cloth will give you a neater tuck. Place your lace insertion length 19 cm (7½″) down centre front. Using DMC ecru thread on your needle, straight stitch lace down.

- Now that you have your centre, use markings on pattern to stitch tucks into place with DMC 4446. Slip the 18 mm (⅝″) edge lace length 19 cm (7½″) under outside tuck, making sure it is against stitching line. Move tuck out of way and straight stitch lace in place. Repeat for other side. If you have any narrow braid or ribbon, stitch down on top of head of lace insertion on both sides, then on stitching line of tucks to give a narrow coloured effect as in diagram. Now you have finished your preparation of your front.

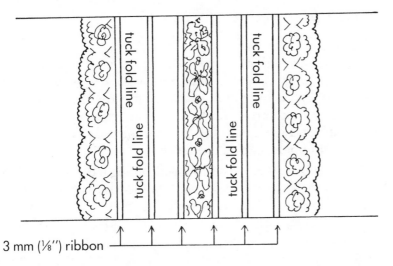

3 mm (⅛″) ribbon

Sequence of lace and tucks

- Place your bodice lining on top, matching centre front line. Cut out your front bodice. Press.
- Using french seams or overlocker, join shoulder seams as in diagram and press. Fold back bodices on fold line and press.

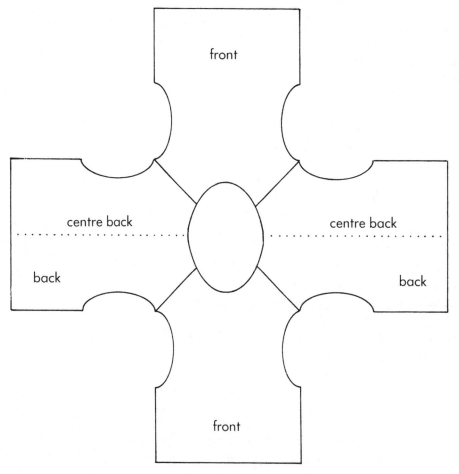

Joining shoulder seams of front and back bodices

- Cut a length of 18 mm (⅝″) edge lace 50 cm (19½″) long. Spray starch and press. Pull up passive thread, fold ends over double. On right side of bodice place lace at centre back fold line and pull up lace to fit around neckline to other centre back fold line. Distribute gathers evenly.
- Straight stitch on seam line, keeping facings free. Place facings right side to right side of bodice and match shoulders; stitch around neckline on previous stitching line. Trim back seam and clip. Turn right side out and press.

- To prepare your sleeves, cut two 19 cm (7½") lengths of insertion. Straight stitch on stitching line of bottom edge of sleeve. Press excess fabric back and on right side, zigzag (W1.5 L1) along head of lace, using method as for underwear. Pull up passive thread in head of insertion.

- Cut two lengths of entredeux 12.5 cm (5") long. Cut away fabric from one side of entredeux and butt gathered insertion lace to fit. Using zigzag W2 L1, stitch together. Repeat for other sleeve.

- Cut two lengths of edge lace 12.5 cm (5") long. Cut away fabric from remaining edge of entredeux and butt edge lace to entredeux using zigzag W2 L1 and stitch in place. Press.

- Run two rows of gathering between markings on sleeve pattern, keeping facings free. Matching shoulder mark on sleeve to shoulder seam and armhole marking, pin sleeve in and pull up gathering to fit armhole, distributing gathers evenly with a little extra gathering at head of sleeve. Stitch sleeve in. Trim back seam.

- Join side seams of bodice and sleeves, making sure laces match. Apply Fray Stoppa or similar fabric glue to ends.

- Join side seams of facings.

SLEEVE EXTENSION

- Cut two pieces of fabric 12.5 cm x 10 cm (5" x 4"). Press.

- Cut six lengths of insertion lace 10 cm (4") long — three for each sleeve extension. Spray starch and press.

- Using method for attaching insertion lace as in bodice, place insertion down centre of extension and again 12 mm (½") each side of centre insertion.

- Cut four lengths of edge lace 12.5 cm (5") long. Spray starch and press. Place length of edge lace 6 mm (¼") from raw edge and straight stitch into head of lace; press back excess fabric and zigzag (W1.5 L1) on head of lace. Cut away excess fabric. Repeat on other extension.

- Place another length 12 mm (½") from fabric edge. Straight stitch in place. Press.

- Join seams, matching laces. Apply Fray Stoppa or similar fabric glue to ends.
- Check length of extension; slip onto arms and put dress on and fit sleeves over extension so that they sit nicely. Measure the required length; you will be slip stitching the extension to entredeux from the right side.
- Mark where sleeve is to come to; trim away any excess, roll and whip edges (using zigzag W3.5 L1), or turn in small hem (whichever you find easiest). Take dress and sleeve extension off and pin in place, matching seams. Slip stitch into entredeux every second hole. Apply Fray Stoppa or similar fabric glue to any loose ends before cutting.

SKIRT

- Mark placket opening down centre back of skirt.
- Slash placket opening.
- Cut a 20 cm (8″) bias strip 4 cm (1½″) wide. Press bias strip in half. With raw edges together, stitch onto placket along stitching line.
- Clip into centre of placket and trim seam.
- Press seam toward bias strip and bring folded edge of bias strip over to meet stitching line on wrong side of skirt. Slip stitch in place.
- Stitch placket together at end as in diagram.
- Run two rows of gathering around waistline of skirt. Mark centre front and sides and match to bodice. Make sure you have left side of placket turned in so it will be concealed when stitching skirt to bodice.
- Pull up gathers to fit bodice. Stitch skirt to bodice, keeping bodice facing free.
- Trim seam and turn under hem on facing and slip stitch to waistline. Clip around sleeves and armhole facing, turn in. Turn hem on armhole facing and slip stitch around.
- Prepare your hem on circular skirt by stitching a length of insertion lace to right side 4 mm (⅛″) inside raw edge. Straight stitch into head of insertion lace, press excess fabric back from lace and, using small zigzag (W1.5 L1), stitch over head of lace on right

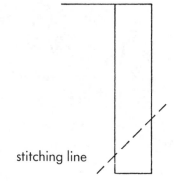

stitching line

Stitch placket together at end

side. Trim away excess fabric. Join ends together. Cut a 3.8 m (4 yd) length of 18 mm (¾″) edge lace; press. Pull up passive thread and gather to fit insertion on hemline.

- Make buttonholes (either by machine or hand). Run Fray Stoppa or similar fabric glue down buttonholes using a pin and let dry. Cut open with embroidery scissors. Sew buttons down centre back.

CAPE

Using cape pattern, cut:
  1 from fabric
  1 from lining

- Transfer markings on pattern for casing onto fabric.
- Place right sides of fabric together, matching top and bottom edge. Stitch 6 mm (¼″) in from raw edge, leaving opening to turn right side out. Turn right side out and press, making sure that lining does not show from right side; slip stitch opening closed.
- Mark stitching lines for casing and straight stitch over these markings, finishing off at each edge. Cut stitches of seam inside casing, just enough to enable you to thread cord through; do not cut close to casing stitches (see diagram).

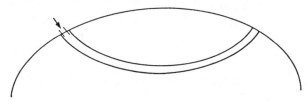

Cut stitches of seam at inside of casing

- Press.
- Cut 1 m (40″) of cord.
- Thread cord through casing. Tie knots at each end of cord 25 mm (1″) from end and pull ends of cord apart to make tassle.
- Using blind hem stitch on your machine and invisible thread, stitch remaining cord around edge of cape, catching fabric edge. Adjust width of stitch to suit cord thickness. Cut away excess cord when finishing off. Apply Fray Stoppa or similar fabric glue to ends of cord.

BAG

Camille's bag is made from strips of embroidered ribbons and cotton laces. By joining these pieces together a rather interesting effect is created. You may like to use the small pieces of ribbon and lace left over from other projects if colours suit.

MATERIALS

- 48 cm (18″) length of 2 cm (¾″) embroidered ribbon, cut into 4 strips of length 12 cm (4½″)
- 48 cm (18″) length of 1.5 cm (½″) embroidered ribbon, cut into 4 strips of length 12 cm (4½″)
- 96 cm (36″) length of 1 cm (⅜″) wide insertion lace, cut into 8 strips of length 12 cm (4½″)
- 44cm (17½″) length of 2 cm (¾″) wide edge lace, cut into 2 strips of 22 cm (8⅝″)
- 69 cm (27″) length of 3mm (⅛″) wide grosgrain or double-sided satin ribbon
- thread to match narrow ribbon for top stitching

METHOD

- Join together alternating strips of embroidered ribbon and lace by butting together using zigzag stitch W1.5 L1.5. Start with a wide piece of embroidered ribbon, then lace, then a narrow piece of embroidered ribbon, then lace, repeating this procedure until all the pieces are joined together.

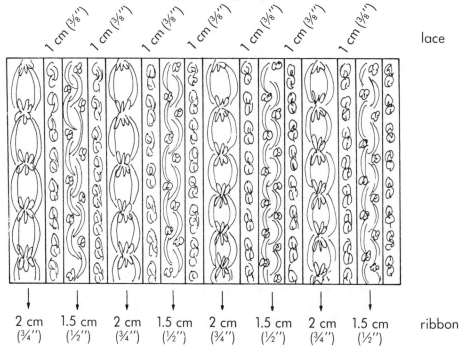

Alternating strips of embroidered ribbon and lace

1 cm (⅜″) 1 cm (⅜″) 1 cm (⅜″) 1 cm (⅜″) 1 cm (⅜″) 1 cm (⅜″) 1 cm (⅜″) lace

2 cm (¾″) 1.5 cm (½″) 2 cm (¾″) 1.5 cm (½″) 2 cm (¾″) 1.5 cm (½″) 2 cm (¾″) 1.5 cm (½″) ribbon

- Stitch one length of edge lace to completed panel, wrong side of lace to right side of one long edge of completed panel.

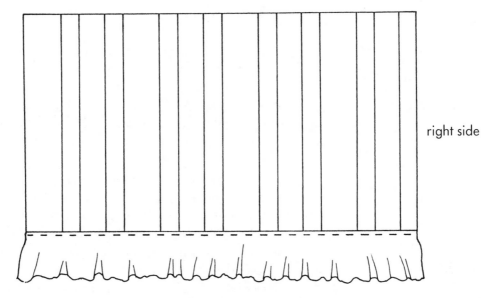

right side

Join length of edge lace to completed panel

- Fold panel, right sides together, and join side seams using small zigzag W1.5 L1.5. Stitch from raw edge through to edge lace.

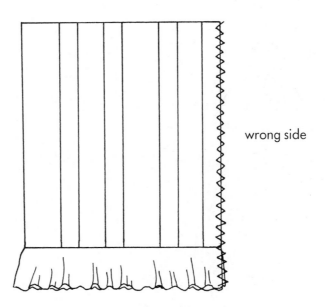

wrong side

Join side seams, right sides together, using small zigzag

- Turn right side out. With fabrics flat together and using straight stitch, stitch into head of edge lace at one end, making sure that you have matched the top and bottom edges together.

- Turn remaining edge under to form a 1 cm (⅜") hem all the way around and straight stitch in place.

- Stitch remaining edge lace piece to the folded hem by butting together using zigzag W1.5 L1.5; overlap the ends of lace.

- Thread elastic through the casing at top of bag, pull up firmly and tie in a double knot. Put a scrunched piece of tulle into the bag to give a fuller effect.

- Cut a 23 cm (9") length of 3 mm width ribbon and place ribbon over the head of lace around the bottom of the bag using a small amount of fabric glue; overlap the ends of the ribbon and cut off any excess. Press ribbon and lace together with fingers and let dry.

- Fold remaining ribbon in half and hand stitch the folded end of ribbon to the inside of the gathered lace at casing. Take both ribbon lengths over to the opposite side of bag to form handle with 16 cm (6¼") of the ribbon. Hand stitch this amount of the ribbon lengths together on the inside of the gathered lace at casing. Separate the remaining lengths of ribbon and tie into a pretty bow to finish off the bag.

Flower circlet and posy are available from doll shops.

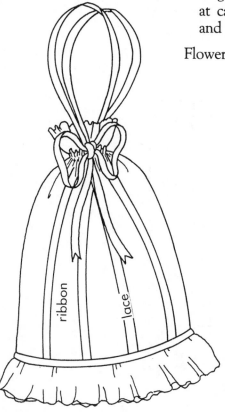

Bag with ribbon handle and bow

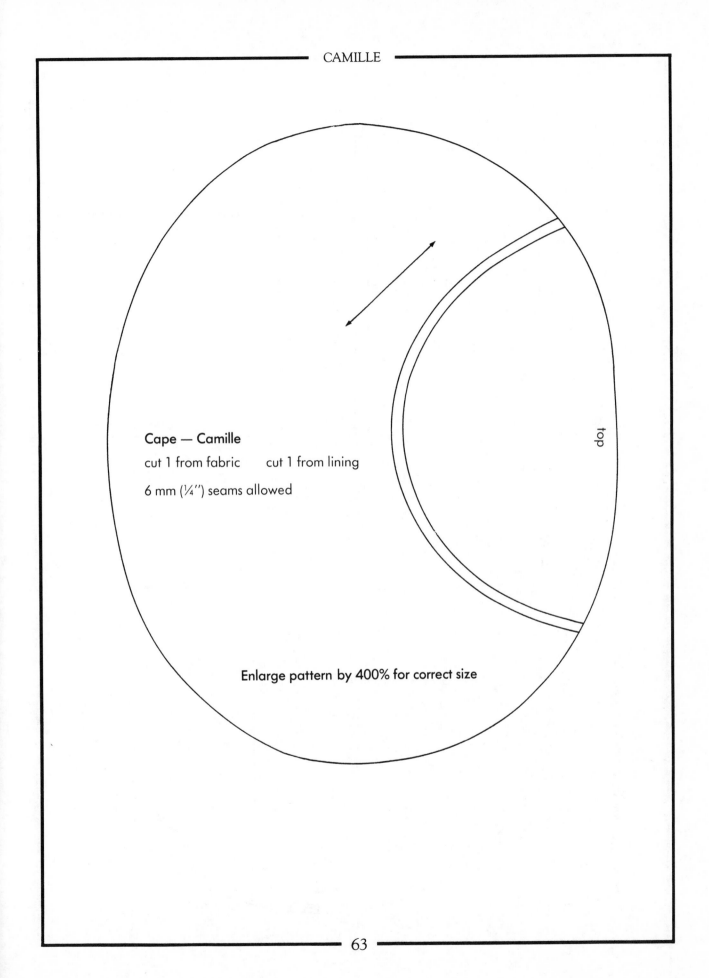

Cape — Camille

cut 1 from fabric   cut 1 from lining

6 mm (¼") seams allowed

top

Enlarge pattern by 400% for correct size

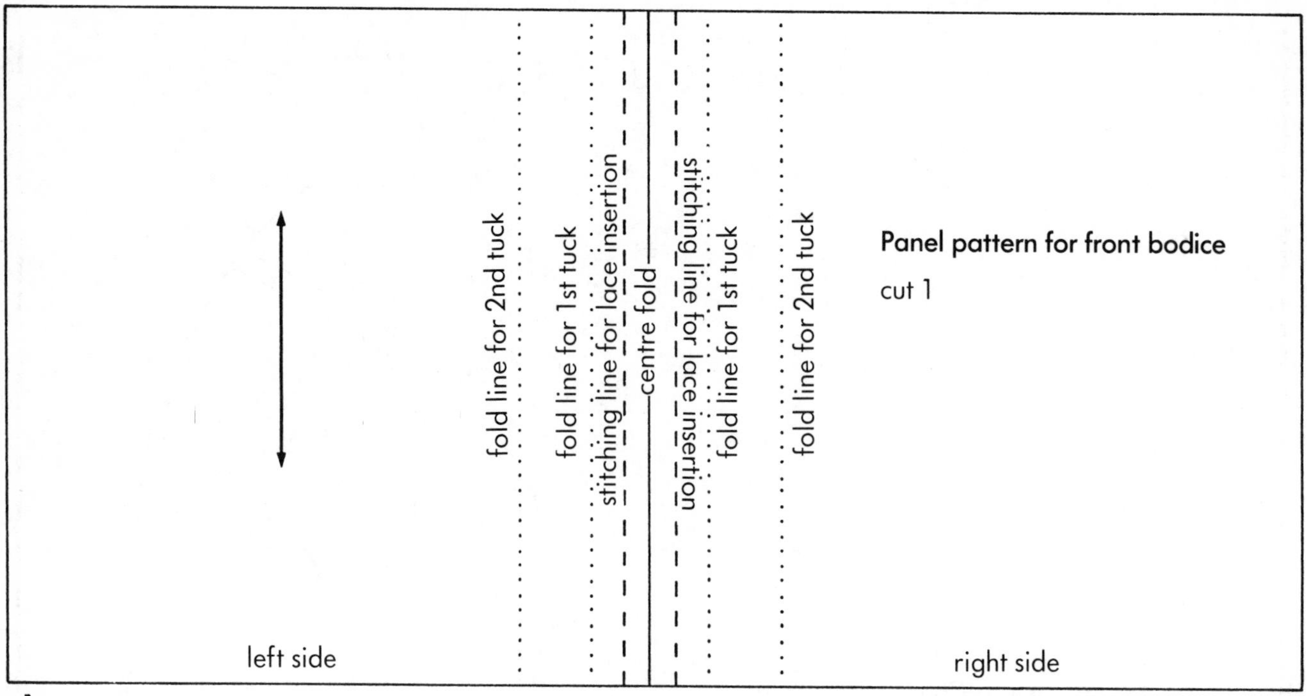

Panel pattern for front bodice

cut 1

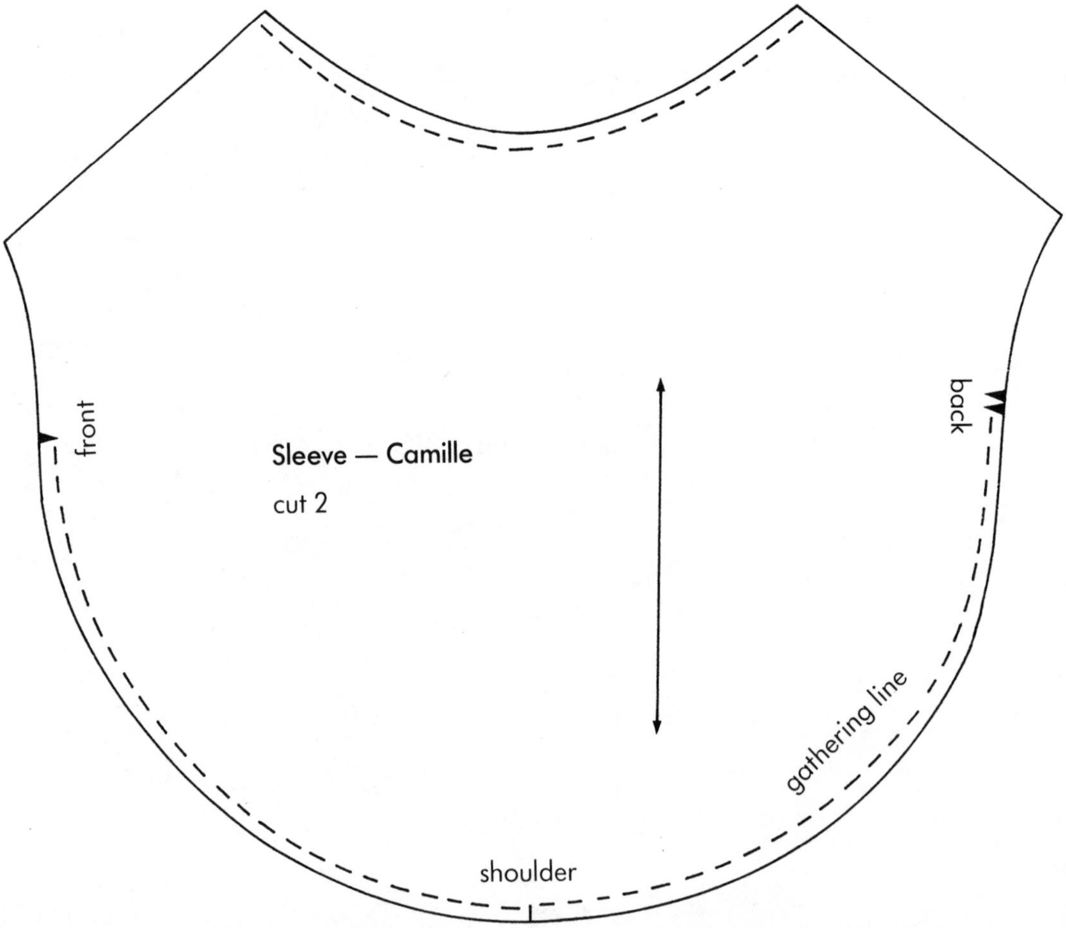

fold line for 2nd tuck

fold line for 1st tuck

stitching line for lace insertion

centre fold

stitching line for lace insertion

fold line for 1st tuck

fold line for 2nd tuck

left side

right side

Enlarge patterns by 200% for correct size

front

back

Sleeve — Camille

cut 2

gathering line

shoulder

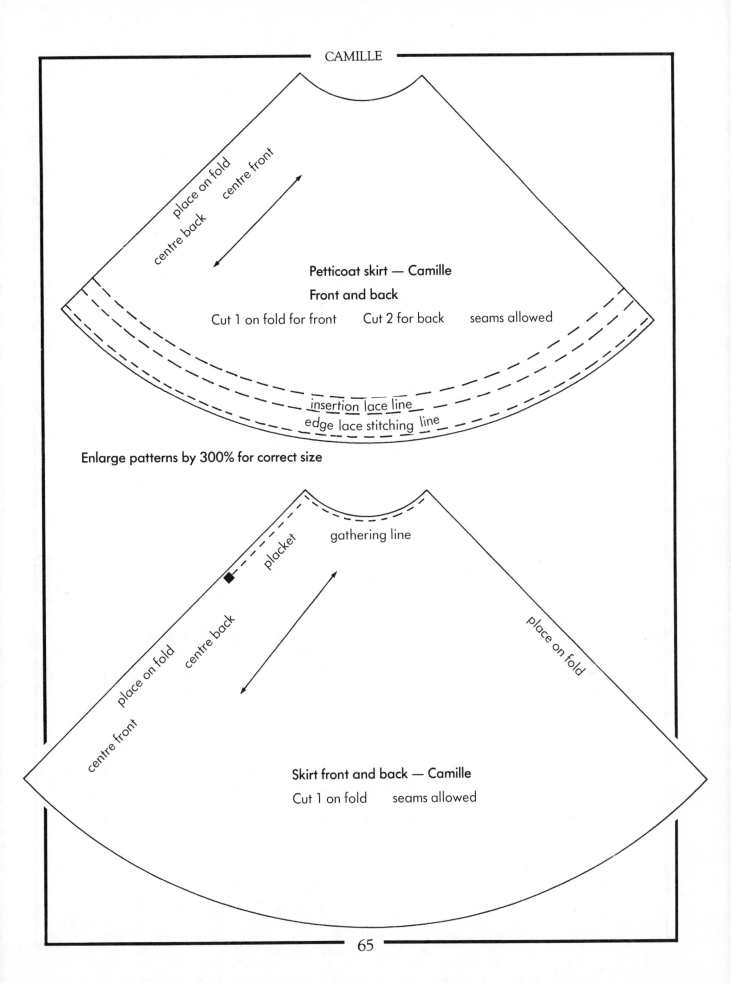

Petticoat skirt — Camille

Front and back

Cut 1 on fold for front   Cut 2 for back   seams allowed

place on fold   centre front

centre back

insertion lace line

edge lace stitching line

Enlarge patterns by 300% for correct size

gathering line

placket

place on fold   centre back

centre front

place on fold

Skirt front and back — Camille

Cut 1 on fold   seams allowed

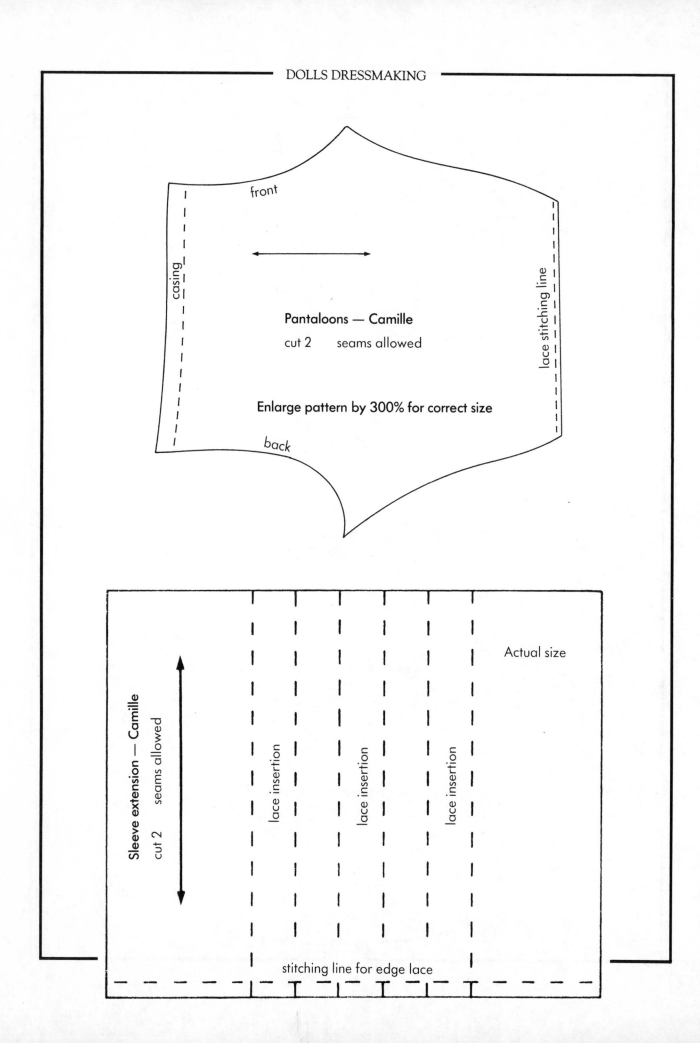

front

casing

lace stitching line

Pantaloons — Camille

cut 2   seams allowed

Enlarge pattern by 300% for correct size

back

Sleeve extension — Camille

cut 2   seams allowed

Actual size

lace insertion

lace insertion

lace insertion

stitching line for edge lace

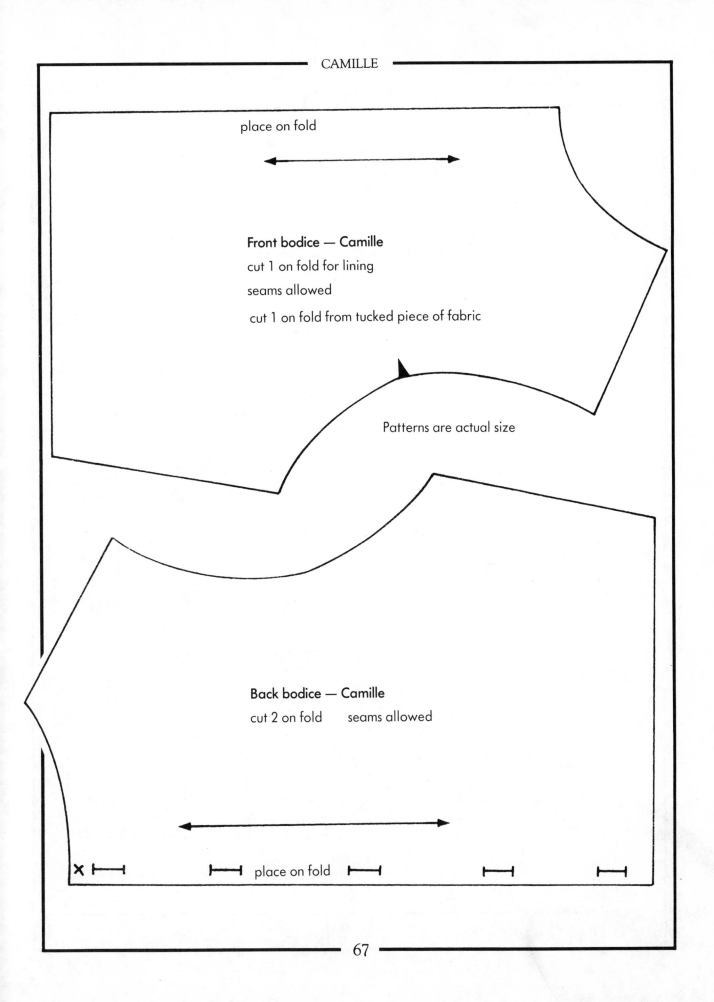

place on fold

Front bodice — Camille

cut 1 on fold for lining

seams allowed

cut 1 on fold from tucked piece of fabric

Patterns are actual size

Back bodice — Camille

cut 2 on fold   seams allowed

X

place on fold

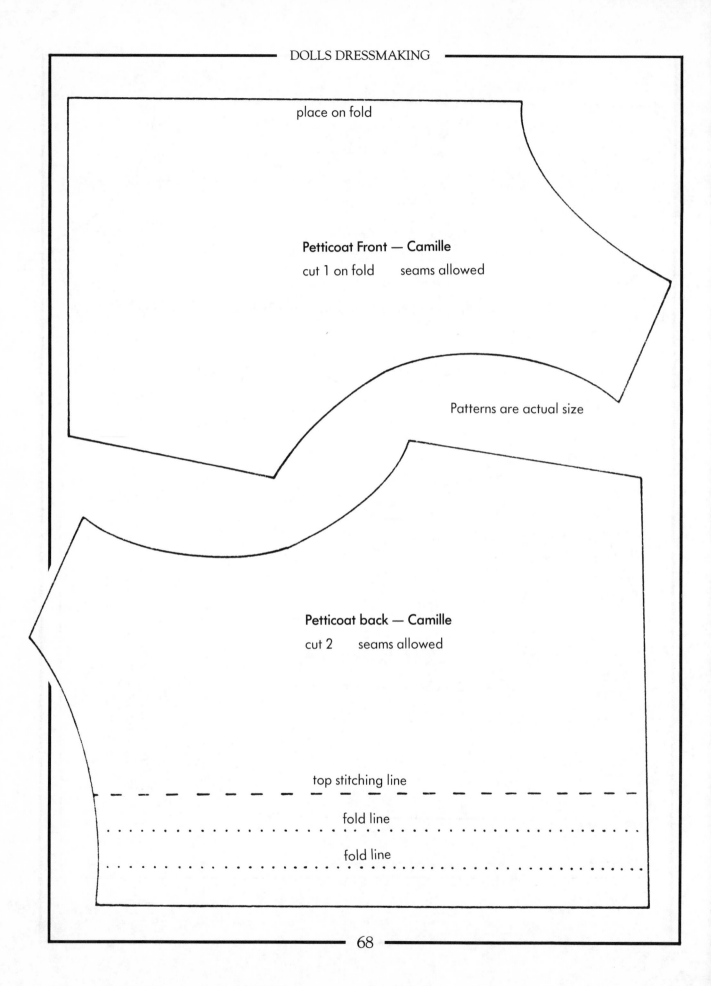

place on fold

Petticoat Front — Camille

cut 1 on fold   seams allowed

Patterns are actual size

Petticoat back — Camille

cut 2   seams allowed

top stitching line

fold line

fold line

CHRISTENING LAYETTE
SLEEPING JENNY —
A 40 cm (16″) DOLL WITH A CLOTH BODY

Deep down we all love baby dolls (some of us a little more than others) and especially appealing is a baby doll dressed in its Christening layette. I have tried to achieve an old-world charm in this layette by using the old fashioned colour ecru, doctor's flannel for the underwear, mother-of-pearl buttons, beautiful embroidery, silk booties and, last but not least, her lovely lace bonnet.

Resting in her covered pram (by Mary McLure), she evokes an era that seems to have warm memories for many people.

FLANNEL UNDERWEAR

MATERIALS

25 cm (10″) doctor's flannel 1.4 m (54″) wide
silk or rayon crochet thread
DMC embroidery thread — colour 3770 ecru
8 x 7 mm (¼″) mother of pearl buttons
wing needle 120/19

METHOD

Using singlet and pilcher pattern, cut:
    1 front singlet
    1 back singlet
    1 pilcher

PILCHERS

• Use a wing needle and stitch 165 W3 L2.5 on the Pfaff 1475CD. (For those using other machines, if you have a stitch that resembles a blanket stitch, this is suitable, if not a zigzag W2.5 L2 can be used.)

- Stitch around raw edges of flannel fabric, making sure you are making a hole in the flannel and also stitching over the raw edge. You may find it easier to stitch with two layers of greaseproof paper underneath the fabric while sewing. Preparing the edge in this way enables you to crochet a silk edge around raw edges.

- Make machine or hand buttonholes on markings on pattern. Use paper underneath fabric when making machine buttonholes. Run Fray Stoppa or similar fabric glue down centre of buttonholes with a pin, let dry and cut with embroidery scissors.

- Sew buttons at markings on pattern.

- Crochet edge, using pattern in crochet section (see p. 84).

- Using DMC embroidery thread colour 3770, stitch your own embroidery design.

SINGLET

- Using french seams or your overlocker set to narrow 3 thread seam, join front to back at side seams, and finish off raw edges. Using your wing needle, stitch around top of singlet as for pilchers to crochet edge.

- Make machine or hand buttonholes at markings on pattern on front shoulders. Run Fray Stoppa or similar fabric glue down middle of buttonholes with pin, let dry and cut with embroidery scissors.

- Sew buttons on back shoulders.

- You may like to crochet around the bottom edge of singlet, or just finish off raw edge with zigzag stitch. I have overlocked my edge with a three thread stitch as it will be tucked in.

- Crochet around top edge — pattern as for pilchers. Using DMC embroidery thread colour 3770 ecru, stitch your own embroidery design.

PETTICOAT

MATERIALS

80 cm (⅞ yd) ecru batiste
2 m (2¼ yds) 35 mm (1²⁄₅″) ecru edge lace
3 small buttons
DMC cotton broder thread size 50 — ecru
1.6/70 twin needle
7 groove pintuck foot for Pfaff machine or whichever
applies to your machine
size 60 machine needle

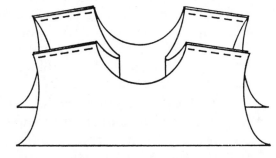

METHOD FOR BODICE

Using bodice yoke pattern, cut:
　2 back yokes on fold
　2 front yokes on fold

Joining shoulders of front to back, including bodice lining

- Join shoulders of fronts to backs, including your bodice lining as in diagram.
- Place wrong sides of fronts together and the backs will automatically fold on fold line. Press.
- Right sides together, matching shoulder seams and fold lines on centre backs, stitch around neckline and armholes. Trim seams and clip as in diagram.
- Turn right sides out by bringing backs through shoulder seams. Press.

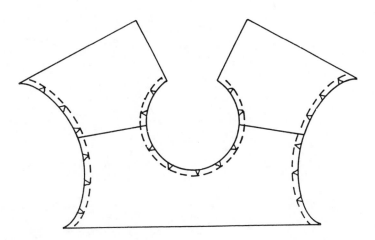

Trim and clip seams of petticoat neckline and armholes

METHOD FOR SKIRT

Using skirt pattern, cut:
  1 back skirt on fold
  1 font skirt on fold

- Join front to back skirt using a french seam on one side only. To do french seams, with wrong sides of fabric together straight stitch 4 mm (⅛″) in from raw edges, trim edges and press seam to one side, then with right sides of fabric. together, straight stitch along outer edge of enclosed seam, making sure you keep previous seam totally enclosed so that no raw edges peep through the final seam. Spray starch and press twice. Join other side seam with a long straight stitch L4-5 as you will remove this when finished pintucking.

- We are now going to pintuck in the round using your pintuck foot — a very quick and easy method. Starting at the side seam (not the french seam), stitch 4 cm (1½″) from the raw edge all the way around until you come back to where you started. Lift your presser foot and move your pintuck to second groove from centre of presser foot. Keep stitching around your skirt — you do not have to stop until you have done enough pintucks — ending at the seam you started on. Always do an odd number of pintucks — 3, 5, 7, 9.

- When you have finished the pintucks, pull out long stitch thread from your temporary seam. Snip threads at line of pintucks. Now you are ready to match pintucks and do the remaining french seam. This method of pintucking is only used on skirts.

- For each armhole, cut a bias strip of fabric 25 mm (1″) wide and stitch it around armhole on right side of fabric. Press seam towards bias strip. Fold over and slip stitch in place by hand.

PLACKET IN SKIRT

- Cut a bias strip of fabric 25 mm (1″) wide and 25 mm (1″) longer than fabric measurement from A to B.

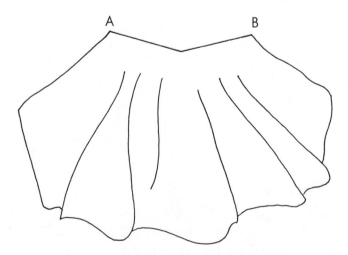

Cut bias strip 25 mm (1″) longer than measurement from A to B

- Cut down centre back line to notch on pattern.
- Fold bias strip in half and press. Place bias strip along slash in back of skirt, right sides together, with the bias strip under the skirt and the raw edges together.
- Stitch from A to B.
- Press seam toward bias strip. Fold over and slip stitch in place by hand.

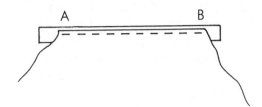

Stitch bias strip to slash in back of petticoat skirt

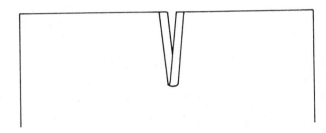

Finished placket

ATTACHING SKIRT TO YOKE

- Run two rows of gathering stitch across the tops of front and back skirts.
- Pin front skirt to front yoke, keeping facing free, and pull up gathers to fit, distributing evenly. Stitch in place.
- Repeat for back skirts, making sure left side of placket is turned in before stitching to skirt.
- Turn under hem on yokes and slip stitch in place by hand.
- Try the petticoat on your baby doll and check the length of the skirt. If length is right, then attach the edge lace to the bottom of the skirt.
- Pick up passive thread in head of lace and pull to gather. You do not want a lot of gathers as it looks too fluffy. Just slightly gather lace and with right sides together, roll and whip (zigzag W3.5 L1) lace to skirt. Roll and whip ends of lace together on wrong side. Use Fray Stoppa or similar fabric glue on all loose threads before cutting away.
- Make machine or hand buttonholes on back yoke corresponding to markings on pattern. Run Fray Stoppa or similar fabric glue down centre of buttonholes with a pin, let dry and cut open with small sharp embroidery scissors.
- Sew small buttons on.

CHRISTENING DRESS

MATERIALS

2 m (2¼ yds) ecru batiste
2.6 m (3 yds) 22 mm (⅞″) edge lace
1.4 m (1½ yds) of 18 mm (¾″) edge lace
3 m (3¼ yds) of 35 mm (1²/₅″) edge lace
2.8 m (3 yds) of 25 mm (1″) insertion lace
3 m (3¼ yds) of 22mm (⅞″) insertion lace
2.6 m (3 yds) of 6 mm (¼″) entredeux
3 small buttons (preferably pearl)
DMC cotton broder thread size 50 — ecru
DMC embroidery thread — colour 739 dark ecru
1.6 m (64″) of 3 mm (⅛″) double-sided satin ribbon

METHOD OF JOINING LACES TO ENTREDEUX

- Spray starch laces and entredeux before joining together.

- Cut one length of 25 mm (1″) insertion lace 12 cm (4¾″) long for centre front of yoke.

- Cut six lengths of 22 mm (⅞″) insertion lace 12 cm (4¾″) long. Cut seven lengths of entredeux 12 cm (4¾″) long.

- Cut away fabric from one side of entredeux and butt to insertion lace; stitch together using zigzag W2 L1.5. Repeat this method until you have joined all your pieces together and you have a lace edge on either side as in the diagram.

Joining laces to entredeux

METHOD FOR CHRISTENING DRESS

From patterns supplied, cut:
   1 front yoke from lace fabric you have put together
   2 back yokes on fold from batiste
   1 front yoke from batiste
   2 sleeves from batiste
   1 front skirt panel from batiste
   2 front skirts from batiste
   1 back skirt on fold from batiste

- Join shoulder seam fronts to backs of yokes and facings using french seams as in petticoat, being careful not to stretch the lace yoke. Press.

- Cut a length of 18 mm (¾") edge lace 40 cm (16") long and pull up passive thread to gather up to fit neck edge.

- Fold ends over double and stitch to right side of yokes from centre back fold line around neckline to other centre back fold line.

- Turn facings right side to right side, stitch around neckline on previous stitching line, clip, turn right sides out and press.

- Join front and back skirts at side seams with french seams; make a placket at centre back of skirt where marked on pattern as for petticoat.

- As you will have a slight shape in your front skirt, we want the lace to take this shape. Using a foam board covered with polycotton fabric, place one front of skirt on board, pin to board and shape lace to fit as follows.

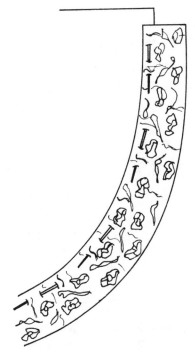

Attaching lace to skirt front

- Cut a 2 m (2¼ yd) length of 25 mm (1") insertion lace. Place lace 6 mm (¼") over raw edge of fabric. Walking your lace from the top edge, pin as you come down the front. As you come nearer the front curve, you will find the lace won't sit; this is where you must shape your lace. Pull passive thread in the head of lace on the left side of lace until you have shaped the lace to fit the curve in the fabric. (Be careful not to break this thread.) When you have the right shape, steam the lace to help it take its proper shape.

- Walk lace across the back of skirt and up the other side of front of skirt.

- Repeat shaping method on the other side of front skirt. Let cool on board.

- Stitch lace to fabric with a straight stitch (L2) into head of lace all the way around. Press excess fabric away from lace. Using zigzag W1.5 L1.5 on right side, stitch over head of lace all the way around. Trim excess fabric away using duck-billed scissors and press.

- Spray starch the front panel and press.

- Using lace insertion measurements indicated on front panel skirt pattern, cut laces and entredeux to the required lengths.

- Cut away fabric from one side of entredeux and butt to lace using zigzag W2 L1. Cut away other side of entredeux fabric and butt to another piece of lace. Repeat this procedure for the other lace insertion.

- Cut wider insertion lace for bottom edge of panel. Place insertion lace 6 mm (¼″) over raw edge and straight stitch (L2) together. Press excess fabric back and zigzag over head of insertion lace. Cut away excess fabric and press.

- Place your finished lace to entredeux pieces on your fabric panel at required widths indicated on panel pattern. Pin in place. Straight stitch into head of lace on outside edges. Slit fabric down centre, being careful not to cut into lace, and press back to either side. Zigzag (W1.5 L1.5) over head of lace. Cut away excess fabric.

- Repeat this procedure for other pieces.

- Press panel when finished attaching lace pieces.

- Place your skirt fronts 6 mm (¼″) over each side of your finished panel, matching shaped section. Straight stitch into head of lace, press excess fabric back and zigzag (W1.5 L1.5) over head of lace. Cut away excess fabric and press.

- Cut entredeux length 1.5 m (60″) and join ends together, laying one end on top of other and overlapping 6 mm (¼″). Stitch together with small close zigzag (W1 L.5).

- Cut away fabric from one side of entredeux. Butt to insertion lace using zigzag W2 L1. Cut away remaining fabric from entredeux. Cut a 3 m (3¼ yd) length of 35 mm (1²⁄₅″) edge lace. Join ends together using roll and whip method (i.e. zigzag W3.5 L1). Pull up passive thread (being careful not to break thread) to fit bottom edge of skirt.

- Butt this edge lace frill to entredeux using zigzag W2.5 L1, adjusting the gathers as you go.

- Cut two lengths of 22 mm (⅞″) edge lace 1 m (40″) long. Spray starch and press. Pull up passive thread in head of lace and place straight edge of lace to outside curve of insertion lace on skirt front as in diagram.

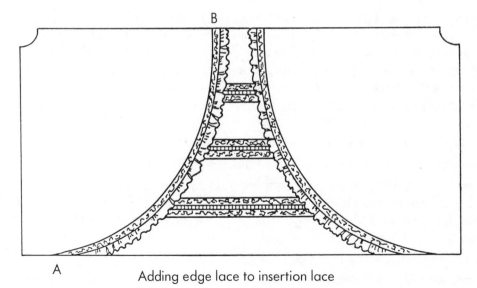

Adding edge lace to insertion lace

- Turn one end of edge lace under and secure, place this end at bottom end of curve (A) and gather to fit around curve up to top of skirt (B).
- Zigzag (W1.5 L1.5)on top of previous zigzag on insertion lace. Press skirt.
- Run two rows of gathering stitches along top of front and back skirts, one row 12 mm (½″) from raw edge; the other row 6 mm (¼″) from raw edge.
- Pull these threads up to fit front yoke and back yokes, making sure you have turned the placket in on left side (and keeping facings free). Stitch between the rows of gathering stitches. Neaten seams.

SLEEVES

- Cut two lengths 20 cm (8″) long of 22 mm (⅞″) insertion lace for ends of sleeves. Spray starch and press.
- Place lace 6 mm (¼″) in from raw edge of sleeve. Straight stitch together along head of lace, press excess fabric back and zigzag (W1.5 L1.5) over head of lace.
- Cut two lengths of entredeux 12 cm (4¾″) long, trim away fabric from one side of entredeux, pull up passive thread in head of lace insertion and gather to fit entredeux.

- Butt entredeux to insertion lace on sleeve, using zigzag W2.5 L1. Cut away remaining fabric from entredeux.
- Cut two lengths of 22 mm (⅞″) edge lace 25 cm (10″) long. Spray starch and press. Pull up passive thread in head of lace to gather to fit entredeux. Butt edge lace frill to entredeux using zigzag W2.5 L1. Repeat for other sleeve.
- Press sleeves and join seams of sleeves using french seams, starting from lace edge to underarm, making sure your laces match.
- Run two rows of gathering stitches between notches on head of sleeve. Fit sleeves into armholes, matching underarm seam to skirt side seam markings and centre of sleeve to shoulder seam.
- Pull up gathers to fit and stitch sleeves in, making sure yoke linings are free.
- Finish off raw edges of sleeve seams using the roll and whip method, i.e. zigzag W3.5 L1.
- Pin yoke linings in place, turn under allowances and slip stitch by hand.
- Cut one length of 22 mm (⅞″) edge lace 1 m (40″) long. This lace is to be frilled up to stitch around yokes. Spray starch and press lace.

- Pull up passive thread to gather and fit around yokes from centre back across and over shoulder, across front and around to centre back, following seams.

- Turn ends under double and slip stitch by hand in place along seams, right side of lace to right side of yokes and straight edge of lace on yoke side of seam. Stitching the lace on this way allows it to fall back down without being flat. Apply Fray Stoppa or similar fabric glue to all your loose ends before cutting away.

- Make machine or hand buttonholes down centre back. Run Fray Stoppa down centre of buttonholes with a pin and let dry before cutting with small embroidery scissors.

- Pearl buttons finish off your garment nicely.

- Cut two 30 cm (12″) lengths of 3mm (⅛″) ribbon, and one 1 m (40″) length for bow on yoke.

- Thread ribbon through entredeux on sleeves to pull up to fit wrists. Make a ribbon bow and stitch to centre of front yoke.

- Use your own designs to embroider on your dress. We have used DMC embroidery thread colour 739 for our embroidery.

LACE BONNET

MATERIALS

50 cm (20″) 35 mm (1²⁄₅″) edge lace
1.5 m (60″) 20 mm (⁴⁄₅″) edge lace
70 cm (27½″) 25 mm (1″) insertion lace
84 cm (33″) 20 mm (⁴⁄₅″) insertion lace
1.55 m (61″) 6 mm (¼″) entredeux
1.5 m (59″) 3 mm (⅛″) double-sided satin ribbon
1 m (40″) 15 mm (½″) double-sided satin ribbon
small amount (10 cm/4″) of double-sided satin ribbon
45 cm (18″) of 40 mm (1½″) beading lace
DMC cotton broder thread size 50 — ecru

METHOD

Spray starch laces and entredeux. Cut:

5 x 14 cm (5½″) lengths of 25 mm (1″) insertion lace

6 x 14 cm (5½″) lengths of 20 mm (⅘″) insertion lace

10 x 14 cm (5½″) lengths entredeux

- Using the method of joining lace to entredeux as in bodice of christening dress (p. 74), join lace to entredeux, alternating wider lace and using zigzag W2 L1.

- Thread 3 mm (⅛″) ribbon through lengths of entredeux. Press.

Using bonnet band pattern, cut:

21 cm (8¼″) length of 40 mm (1½″) beading for front band

16 cm (6¼″) length for back band

- Mark seam allowance on ends of back bonnet band as shown in diagram. Press.

12 cm (4¾″)

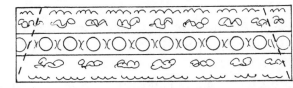

seam allowance   15 cm (6″)   seam allowance

Back bonnet band

- Join back band lace to front lace piece as shown in the diagram, using small straight stitch.

front band

25 mm (1″)   25 mm (1″)

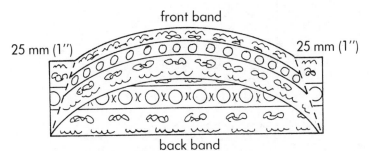

back band

Join back band lace to front band lace

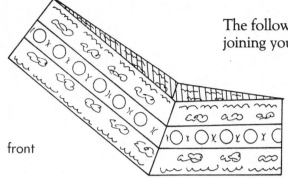

The following diagram shows how it should look after joining your laces.

back

front

Joined laces (side view)

- Press open seams and trim away excess.
- Using bonnet pattern, cut out bonnet from the lace fabric you have previously put together.
- Run two rows of gathering stitch across front of bonnet. Check width against front beading band on stitching line, which will be 6 mm (¼″) from edge.
- Take your 50 cm (20″) length of 35 mm (1²/₅″) edge lace, spray starch and press.
- Pull up passive thread (carefully so it doesn't break) to gather lace to fit across front of bonnet. Place lace wrong side down on to right side of front bonnet 6 mm (¼″) in from edge. Using zigzag W1.5 L1.5, stitch lace down from front corner to other front corner.
- Straight stitch centre back seam, trim, and roll and whip to tidy edges. If using fabric instead of lace, use a french seam.
- Place your beading band on to your bonnet 6 mm (¼″) in from edge, matching corners and centre back.
- Catch frill ends of edge lace into band. Using zigzag stitch W1 L1, stitch around on the 6 mm (¼″) line.

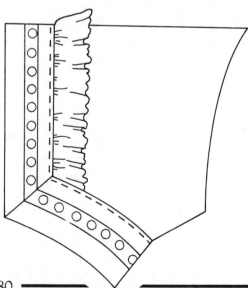

Attaching beading band to bonnet,
catching ends of frilled edge lace into band

- Cut 1 m (40″) length of 20 mm (⅘″) edge lace. Spray starch and press.
- Pull up passive thread and gather to fit outside edge of beading lace. Starting at centre back, using zigzag W1 L1, stitch frilled lace underneath beading lace 6 mm (¼″) in from outside edge.

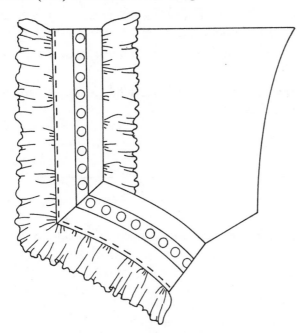

Stitch frilled edge lace underneath beading lace on bonnet

- Thread 3 mm (⅛″) ribbon through beading around band.
- Cut bonnet band lining from fabric using bonnet band pattern. Join at side seams and tidy edges using roll and whip method. Press.
- Pin to wrong side of bonnet, matching fronts and backs and making sure they fit together without stretching lace band.
- Turn under edges and pin; slip stitch lining down on both sides.
- Run two rows of gathering stitches around back opening in bonnet; pull up as far as you can and secure.
- Cut a 10 cm (4″) length of 22 mm (⅞″) edge lace and pull up passive thread in head of lace to form a rosette. Tie off to secure. Hand stitch ends together.
- Place your rosette over the gathered area of the back of the bonnet. Attach by hand, making sure rosette is secure.

- Cut a 10 cm (4″) length of 6 mm (¼″) double-sided satin ribbon and hand stitch, ready to form a ribbon rosette (see diagram).
- Pull thread up to form rosette and secure ends together, place over centre of lace rosette on back of bonnet. Stitch in place.
- Cut small medallion of fabric to cover raw edges of centre of bonnet on the inside, and slip stitch in place.
- Attach ribbon ties at sides, make ribbon rosettes and attach over ribbon ties.
- Apply Fray Stoppa or similar fabric glue to any loose threads before cutting away.

Hand-stitching zigzag on double-sided ribbon to form rosette

CROCHETED SHOES AND BOOTIES

My thanks goes to my mother for the time and patience she has put into these lovely crocheted shoes and booties. My mother remembered her mother crocheting booties and edges for friends when she was a little girl — these are in a way a remembrance of times gone by.

I hope you enjoy making these from the patterns she worked out from memory.

SHOES

MATERIALS

3 ply silk or rayon crochet thread
1.50 mm (No. 7) crochet hook

METHOD

1st row	Make 6 ch, join with slip stitch
2nd row	16 d.c. into ring
3rd row	6 d.c. (chain 3, miss 2 d.c., 2 d.c.) repeat twice — join with a slip stitch
4th row	6 d.c. (6 d.c. into ch loop, 2 d.c.) three times
5th row	d.c. in every stitch
6th row	d.c. to last 6 d.c. make 36 ch, join to first d.c.
7th row	d.c. in rounds for 7 rows

Shaping of soles:

decrease 1 d.c., each side of centre 6 d.c., continue to back, leaving 2 d.c. in centre and decreasing 1 d.c. each side

Continue decreasing in the same manner for 5 rounds

Join sole with slip stitch

Work a picot st around top

Make an ankle strap with 11 ch, turn 1 dc into 3rd stitch from hook (this makes buttonhole), continue in d.c. to end

Work rose buds at base of medallion

BOOTIES

MATERIALS

3 ply silk or rayon crochet thread
1.50 mm (No. 7) crochet hook

METHOD

1st row	Make 60 ch, join into a circle
2nd row	d.c. round and join
3rd row	1 d.c., miss 1 d.c., 3 tr into next d.c. (shell forms), miss 1 d.c., 1 d.c. into next d.c. * repeat and join
4th row	3 tr into first d.c., 1 d.c. into centre tr of shell, repeat around and join
5th—7th row	Repeat 4th row

Shape front:

1st row	Shell pattern to centre front, 4 shells, 1 d.c. into the centre tr of each shell (6 decreases), turn, 1 d.c. into 6 d.c., continue in d.c. to end and join
2nd row	Complete 1 more row of shells around and join
3rd row	1 tr, 1 ch into centre tr of each shell and d.c. (ribbon holes)
4th row	Finish with tr, picot, 2 tr into first loop, 1 d.c. into next loop, continue to end, join
Sole	Join silk and continue d.c., decreasing 1 d.c. each side of centre, 6 d.c. at front, decrease 1 d.c. each side of 2 d.c. at back. Repeat for 4 rows
5th row	Decrease every second d.c. to end of row.

Join sole with slip stitch.

CROCHET EDGE PATTERN FOR EDGING
AROUND FLANNEL SINGLET AND FLANNEL PILCHERS

MATERIALS

3 ply silk or rayon crochet thread
1.50 mm (No. 7) crochet hook

METHOD

Pattern consists of one row.
2 d.c., 3 ch, slip stitch into 1st ch, 2 d.c., 3 ch, slip stitch into 1st ch. Repeat around garment.

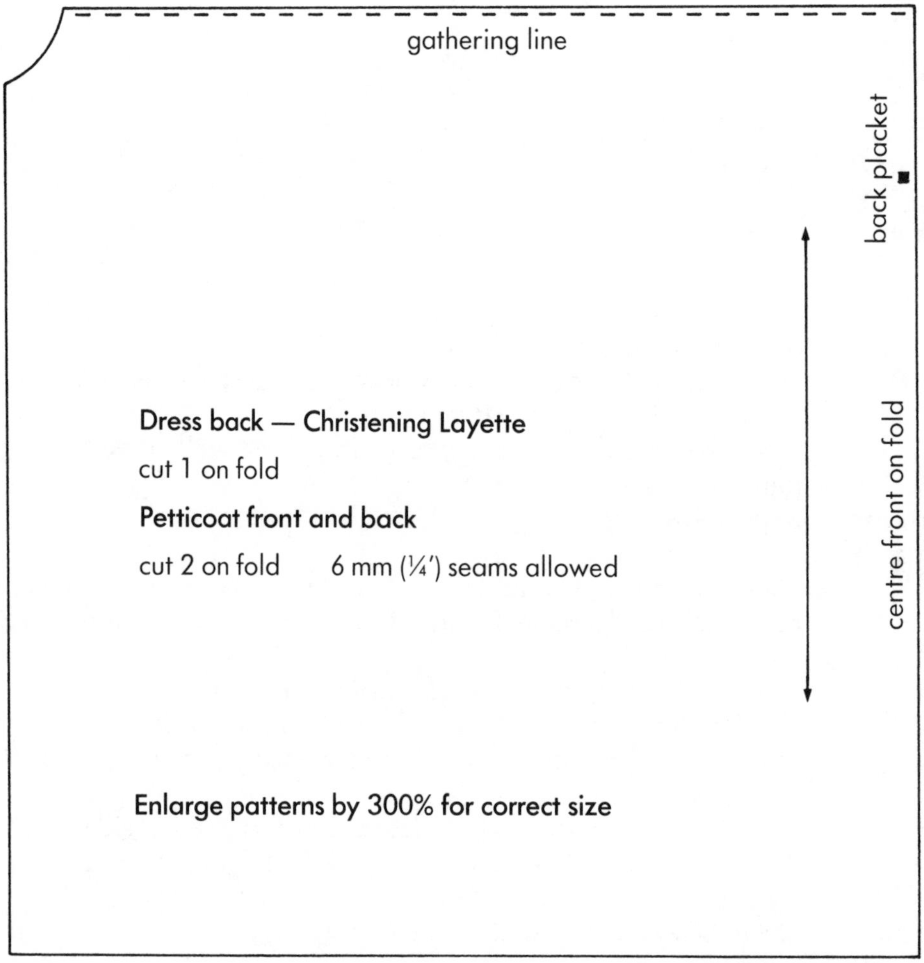

gathering line

back placket

centre front on fold

Dress back — Christening Layette

cut 1 on fold

Petticoat front and back

cut 2 on fold   6 mm (¼') seams allowed

Enlarge patterns by 300% for correct size

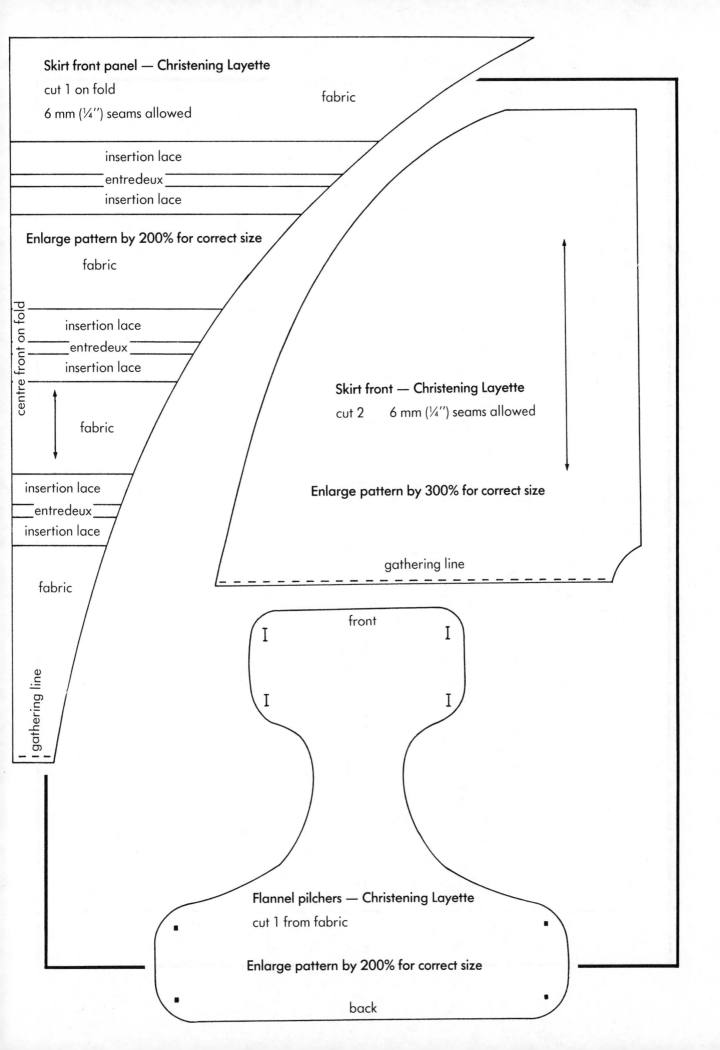

Skirt front panel — Christening Layette

cut 1 on fold

6 mm (¼'') seams allowed

fabric

insertion lace

entredeux

insertion lace

Enlarge pattern by 200% for correct size

fabric

centre front on fold

insertion lace

entredeux

insertion lace

fabric

insertion lace

entredeux

insertion lace

fabric

gathering line

Skirt front — Christening Layette

cut 2   6 mm (¼'') seams allowed

Enlarge pattern by 300% for correct size

gathering line

front

Flannel pilchers — Christening Layette

cut 1 from fabric

Enlarge pattern by 200% for correct size

back

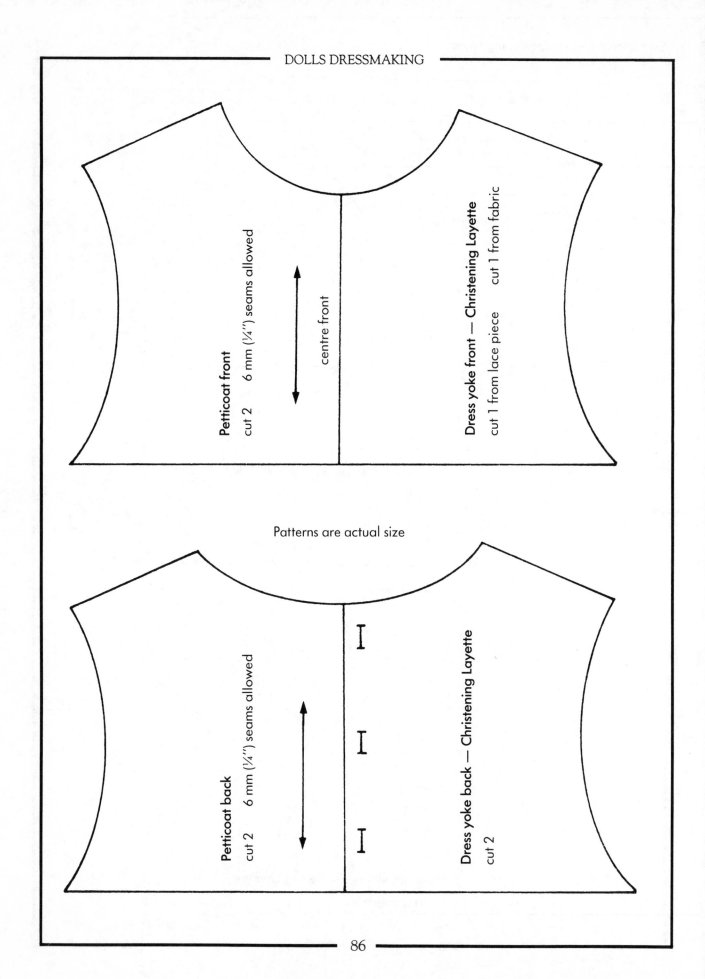

Petticoat front

cut 2   6 mm (¼") seams allowed

centre front

Dress yoke front — Christening Layette

cut 1 from lace piece   cut 1 from fabric

Patterns are actual size

Petticoat back

cut 2   6 mm (¼") seams allowed

Dress yoke back — Christening Layette

cut 2

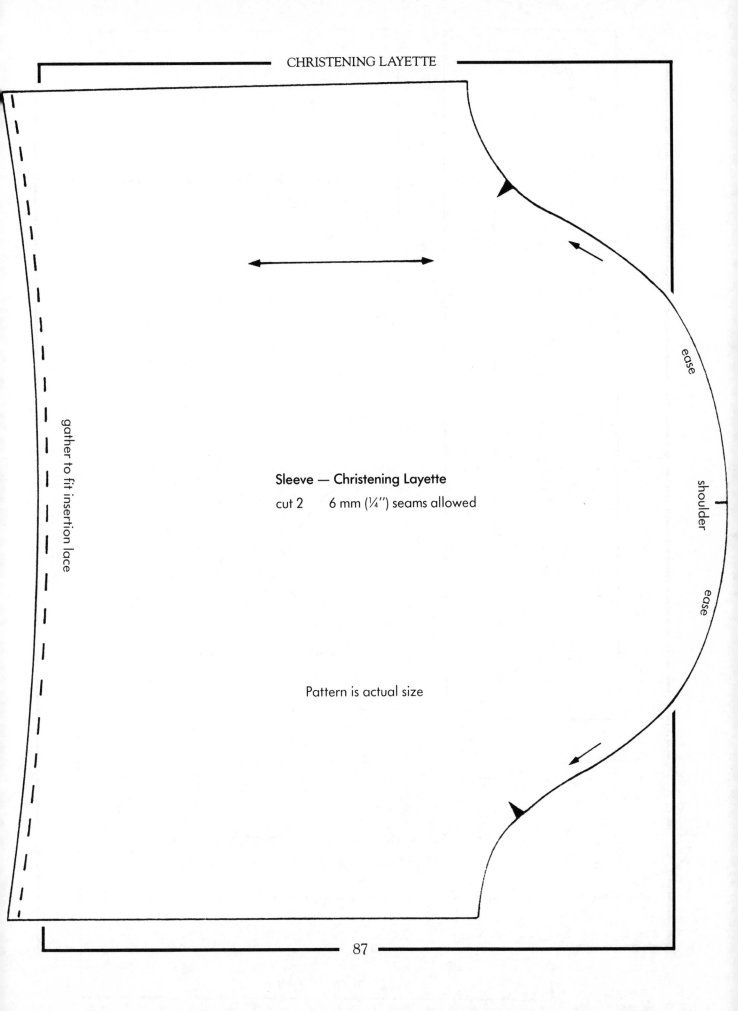

gather to fit insertion lace

Sleeve — Christening Layette

cut 2   6 mm (¼") seams allowed

Pattern is actual size

ease

shoulder

ease

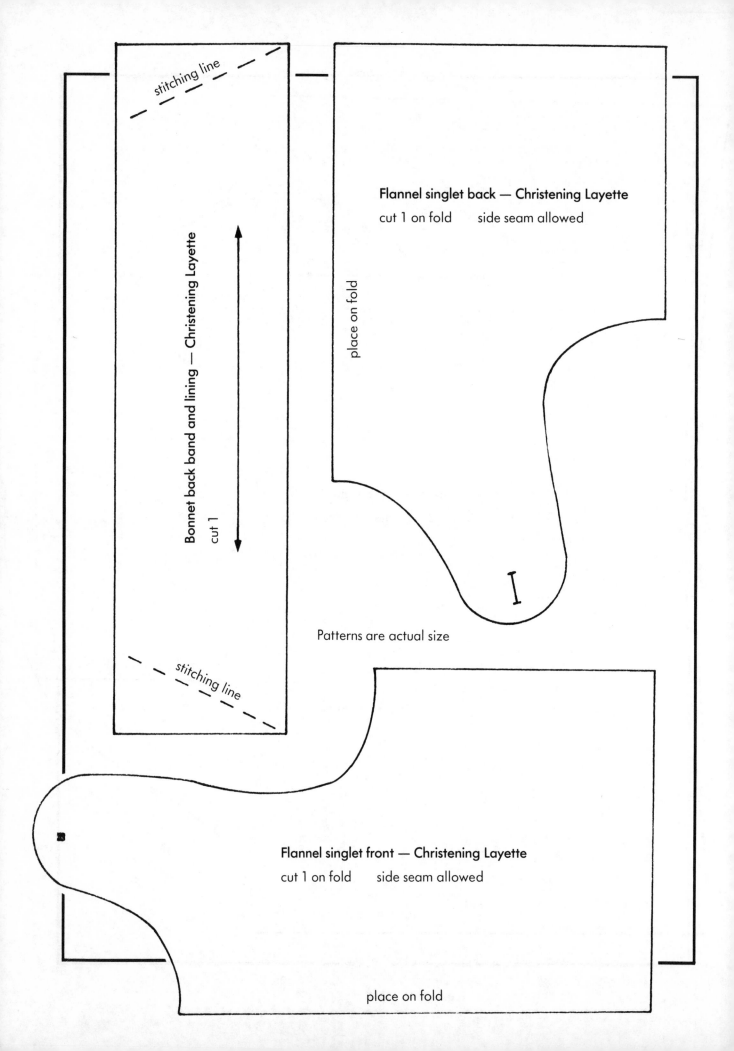

stitching line

Flannel singlet back — Christening Layette

cut 1 on fold   side seam allowed

place on fold

Bonnet back band and lining — Christening Layette

cut 1

Patterns are actual size

stitching line

Flannel singlet front — Christening Layette

cut 1 on fold   side seam allowed

place on fold

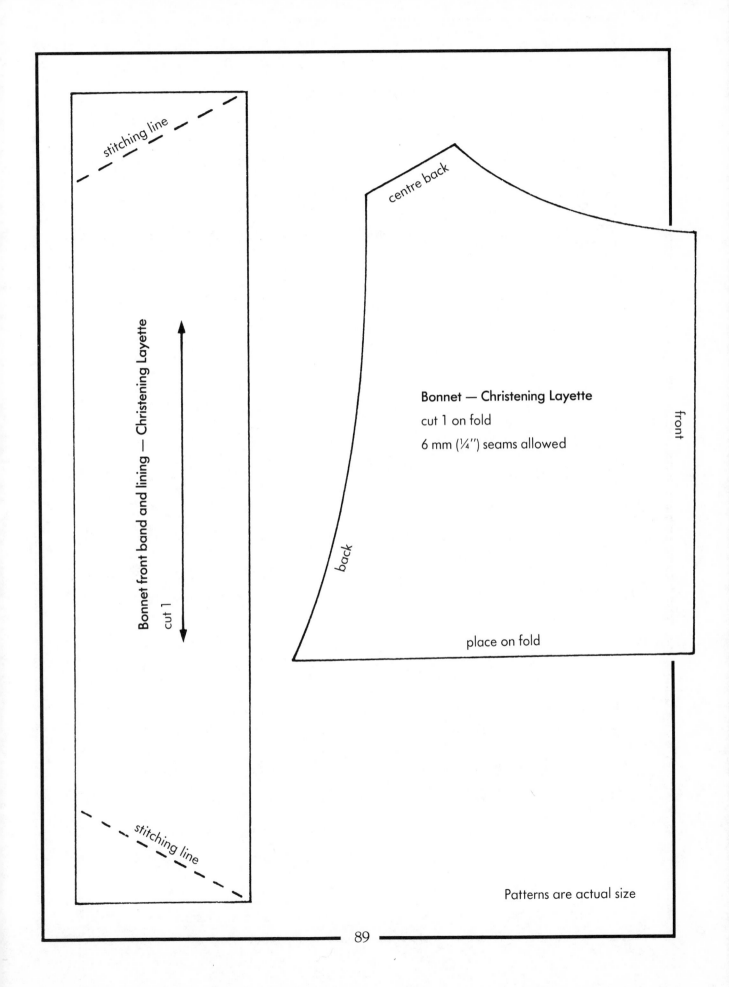

stitching line

Bonnet front band and lining — Christening Layette

cut 1

stitching line

centre back

back

Bonnet — Christening Layette

cut 1 on fold

6 mm (¼″) seams allowed

front

place on fold

Patterns are actual size

ENLARGING PATTERNS

A simple method to enlarge those patterns requiring enlargement is to use a reducing and enlarging photocopier.

- Where the enlargement required is 200%, most photocopiers will enlarge to this size.

- Where the enlargement required is 300%, first enlarge to 200%, then enlarge that by 150%.

- Where the enlargement required is 400%, first enlarge to 200%, then enlarge that by 200%.